I0819368

FREEDOM

FREEDOM

Zinzi Clemmons

VIKING

VIKING
An imprint of Penguin Random House LLC
1745 Broadway, New York, NY 10019
penguinrandomhouse.com

"The Suburban Strategy" appeared, in slightly different form, in *The Baffler*, issue no. 59 (2021).

DESIGNED BY MEIGHAN CAVANAUGH

LIBRARY OF CONGRESS CONTROL NUMBER: 2026008370
ISBN 9780735221741 (hardcover)
ISBN 9780735221758 (ebook)

Printed in the United States of America
1st Printing

The authorized representative in the EU for product safety and compliance is Penguin Random House Ireland, Morrison Chambers, 32 Nassau Street, Dublin D02 YH68, Ireland, https://eu-contact.penguin.ie.

For André and Marcel

In the realm of human affairs, we know the author of the "miracles." It is men who perform them—men who because they have received the twofold gift of freedom and action can establish a reality of their own.

—Hannah Arendt, "What Is Freedom?"

The most potent weapon in the hands of the oppressor is the mind of the oppressed. If one is free at heart, no man-made chains can bind one to servitude.

—Steve Biko, "Black Consciousness and the Quest for a True Humanity"

CONTENTS

AUTHOR'S NOTE

I had gone in search of a man-killing wolf called slavery; to my dismay I kept finding the tracks of a lamb called freedom.

—Orlando Patterson, *Freedom in the Making of Western Culture*

I came of age in the 1990s in southeastern Pennsylvania, surrounded by a strong community of South African expats and traveling frequently to Johannesburg, where the idea of freedom—lofty yet close enough to taste—was all around. Friends and loved ones kept up breathlessly with the events at home (home was always South Africa, no matter how many years one lived abroad). In our trips to Joburg to visit my family, *amandla!*—"power!" in Zulu—and the songs of gumboot dancers animated our lives. It all culminated in 1994, when my mother and her friends were able to vote for the first time in the country's first all-race elections, and not long after that, Nelson Mandela was elected the nation's first black president.

In subsequent years, and still to this day, freedom lived in the complicated legacy of Nelson Mandela. Mandela at once embodies the hopes and traumas of black people in South Africa—and of many post-independence Africans as well—and also the concessions that were deemed necessary in order to gain said independence, which ended up further entrenching white economic power and black poverty.

These essays reflect a world buckling under the consequences of centuries of interlocking injustices, to be borne by the younger generations, which grows increasingly precarious as time passes. Of those that follow, "Freedom" was written first, in 2014, which began from a consideration of the dangers and complications that are mostly unimagined in the struggle to become free. This idea turned out to encompass the freedom of adulthood and that of nations that have, after many trials, achieved independence.

In 2024, Mandela's ruling African National Congress (ANC) party finally lost its majority control of government for the first time in thirty years, after facing strong challenges from the liberal Democratic Alliance (mostly backed by Afrikaans-speaking whites and coloureds) and from former members-turned-insurgents Jacob Zuma and his MK Party and Julius Malema and his Economic Freedom Fighters (EFF). South Africans had been disillusioned by the ANC for years due to the party's corruption and its inability to deliver on the promises of independence. This was at no time more obvious than in the wake of Mandela's passing, when a new generation born after independence (the so-called Born Frees) came of age with new and higher demands of their leaders.

I began writing around the time I finished my first novel, *What We Lose*, which fictionalized an experience I had in my twenties—the death of my mother. "Freedom" was an effort to write about its aftermath in nonfiction. The essay attempts to deal with the wake of such a huge, self-defining event as the loss of one's parent, and losing a parent such as the one I did—dominant, controlling, frustrating, caring, beautiful, complex, as all the most interesting humans are. Such humans we call characters, and she surely was one.

The remaining essays that make up this book were written after I'd begun to reflect explicitly on the nature of freedom. The idea resounds in "Freedom, Pt. 2," which captures the fate that often befalls women who have the audacity to be free. The essay looks at how experiencing sexual harassment early in my career formed my views on gender equality. It is also the story of the painful fallout of one these events in the harsh glare of the public eye.

The struggle for economic justice in the form of desegregation has defined much of the last few decades for African Americans. Housing and educational segregation invisibly circumscribed my childhood in Pennsylvania, a phenomenon I became lucidly aware of only years after leaving. As I worked on "Chasing Robbie"—about the loss of a dear childhood friend and how his death was, in a sense, predetermined by segregation—the unequal funding of school districts in Pennsylvania was declared unconstitutional in a lawsuit brought by several bodies, including parents' rights groups, five school districts, and the National Association for the Advancement of Colored People (NAACP). My family used to live within one of those districts, William Penn, and moved away because of its underperformance. The court decision was a victory for Pennsylvanian children and families, and for educators like Robert Payne, who spent his last years trying to right the imbalance inflicted by decades of unjust practices.

Barack Obama occupies a similar, though less pivotal, position to Mandela for black Americans. Obama's election in 2008 marked a parallel turning point in my life. At once a symbol of hope and progress, his failings in the aftermath of the recession—specifically to aid the working class in favor of big banks and finance, leaving black Americans more disadvantaged than before—helped set the stage for many of the problems of post-2016 America. The shattering of my hope, and the reckoning with the betrayal of a former hero, is a theme throughout this book. This experience drove me deeper into radicalism, defining much of the next decade of my life. "A People Without a Nation" reflects on that journey, which parallels a larger struggle in black intellectualism.

Freedom is an idea that defines Western societies, but its meaning, as noted by decades of scholars, is vague and often taken for granted. Enter Jamaican sociologist Orlando Patterson (an important figure in "A People Without a Nation"), who offers a compelling definition in his landmark 1991 study, *Freedom*, vol. 1: *Freedom in the Making of Western Culture.* In it, he argues that freedom is socially constructed and inhabits three forms: personal freedom (the most elementary), the ability to not be restrained or coerced; sovereignal freedom, the ability to pursue one's desires; and civic freedom, the ability to participate in the governance of a community or state.

For the American right, freedom has always been narrowly confined to the single-minded pursuit of sovereignal freedom at the complete expense of other people's. Look no further than their bloodthirsty drive to eliminate LGTBQ and abortion rights in the name of "religious freedom." In the hands of an increasingly extreme and repressive ruling class, the term loses all meaning. These are the delusional rantings of people so drunk with privilege as to not notice that they are already free. I hope to push back against this limited notion of freedom, which has been used over time to enslave, murder, and subjugate countless others. In this book, I encounter such mythology in the American West ("Home Going")—the site of their fantasies of westward expansion—and in the figure of Donald Trump ("The Suburban Strategy").

On the contrary, for black people, the notion of freedom is expansive, revised continually over time through generations of struggle and triumph. In South Africa, this idea echoed in the Mozambiquan slogan *A luta continua!*—"The struggle continues!" in Portuguese—later sung by Miriam Makeba and heard often in my childhood. It is within this expansive vision, rooted in struggle, born in the African diaspora, that this book is forged.

As I finish this book in late 2025, the question of freedom seemingly acquires new urgency, as fascism rises worldwide, dissent and protest are increasingly crushed, and the United States veers into authoritarianism. While we struggle to preserve our rights, we recognize that Western liberal democracies sowed the seeds of their demise through militarism and hypercapitalism (and the unholy alliance of the two); in slavery and apartheid; in the scramble for Africa; in the War on Drugs and the War on Terror. At the same time, the Global South rises to challenge their hegemony. World war, of the type we saw almost exactly one century ago, at times feels inevitable. The horror of Gaza is not only inherent in its brutality and speed, but in the knowledge that it replicates the cruelty of centuries of colonial violence, supercharged and livestreamed all over the world. It is a proxy battle (like Ukraine and Russia) of the direct confrontation between the imperial West and the Global South that is only beginning to unfold.

In this moment of great peril, politicians have become less responsive to the people. The haves and the have-nots, the governing and the governed, grow further apart. Debate rages over how to solve the problem of today's politics: which party, political figure, economic proposal, legislation, and so on will save us from ourselves. The solution is so obvious as to go unremarked. The opposite of authoritarianism is democracy. More democracy. More freedom, not less. Assuring the rights of *all* people in society—not only our civic freedoms but the freedom from poverty, poor health, police violence, surveillance, climate disaster; the right to individualism and expression: to say, be, and love whomever we want, without censure, forever in perpetuity.

It is to the eternal notion of struggle and the constant pursuit of freedom that we must turn. As Patterson writes, "Who were the first persons to get the unusual idea that being free was not only a value to be cherished but the most important thing that someone could possess? The answer, in a word: slaves."

It is up to the world to listen.

SWAN SONG FOR THE REPUBLIC

We are born into good times. "Dream big," they tell us. "The sky's the limit."

We are lied to.

One day at school, I'm shepherded into the band practice room, the TV set rolled out of the closet and switched on. On the screen I see smoke billowing from familiar buildings, the broken body of a plane in an empty field, reporters screaming, everything veiled in dust.

We start to fear.

The whispers of war crescendo and no one seems to realize that the people who attacked us don't come from the small country we now wish to invade. I sneak onto my family's computer and read article after article, trying to make sense of what we are about to do, but it can't be made sense of.

Liza and I cut class and load into my mother's car, certain we are about to change the world. When we show up, there are just a handful of people shouting slogans at harried passersby on their way home from work. We return to where our car was parked to find it has been towed. My mother picks us up from the impound lot across town and drives us back to the suburbs in silence.

We are too young to know better.

My parents manage to save enough for college. The money is the accumulation of so many years, missed dinners and band recitals. It's swallowed whole; the rest I will pay in parcels for the foreseeable future, the total sacrifice unknown. But I needn't worry, I'm told, my future is bright and my dreams will all come true.

We sign on the dotted line.

In the exit counseling session, just before graduation, we're taught about the dangers of default—wage garnishment, impacted credit score, imprisonment, depression, anxiety, loneliness, death . . .

I manage to earn enough for my expenses with nothing left over. My friends work in retail and tutor and crowd their parents' basements. I couch surf with relatives and then pay my friend's mother two hundred dollars a month to live in his little sister's bedroom, under a pink comforter, with her basketball trophies and stuffed animals gazing upon me.

One day at work, I see bankers carrying boxes down the elevator of my twenty-story office building, a look of terror and exhilaration in their eyes. The markets have crashed; the bankers take off like bandits.

We are easy marks, open targets.

All of my friends lose what few jobs they have, their parents' companies fold, childhood homes are foreclosed. I recall the small, scared look of my father—the only black man in his division—when his company announced layoffs.

But something is stirring in this country. There's a name on the lips of our friends.

Years ago, he spoke at my college, and on the day tickets were given out, the line stretched from the box office clear across the main quad. I snuck into the building before the event began and crouched behind the wall of the balcony. I listened to him speak.

My friends take jobs on his campaign and move to towns I've never heard of. The night of the election I go to my neighborhood bar, the place that plays old-school hip-hop on Thursdays and golden soul on Fridays. When the result is announced we scream and embrace each other; I call my parents breathlessly, text disbelief to my friends. We rush out onto the street, to sidewalks packed with strangers of every color; a bus drives by and inside, lit up, all the passengers are dancing.

We let ourselves hope.

I go to graduate school. My friends find new jobs, and I find new friends. I put money away, but it is always eaten up. The city becomes too expensive, so I move to a smaller city, and when that becomes unaffordable, I move to the countryside. Then to another coast. Our lives are shuffled around in boxes and, in between self-storage lockers and garages, some items are lost in transit. A paperback lovingly creased and annotated, a photo of long-gone friends, a family heirloom.

We learn to let go of our attachments to material things.

More murders are publicized, more every year, so many that they begin to punctuate our lives. I hear news of a teenager in Florida, killed walking through his family's neighborhood, and it brings our parents' warnings to life. How could that face mean anything but innocence to anyone?

Our outrage becomes mundane and soon we don't even realize we are numb.

When the country elects a reality-TV star we are shocked but not surprised. When I lived in the countryside, I saw white people living in rusty trailers and broken-down shacks, saw their anger at being left behind. One of them asked me to my face, *Why would you want to live here*? I had no reply, unsure of how to explain that I'd been disappointed, too.

We realize we've been sold false hope.

I go away one weekend and return home to find the grocery store completely emptied out, nothing at all left on the shelves—a zombie movie come to life. I sell off everything that won't fit in my car, load in my husband, my dog, and the handful of belongings we still hold dear: my mother's wedding ring, an old teapot, a flower pressed between glass.

We spend months indoors, watch the world reorient around a new, darker loneliness. Every day, someone dies, and sometimes it is someone we know. We live side by side with death, begin to see it everywhere. We cry until we can't anymore, drink until we make ourselves sick. The world expands and contracts, and I contemplate which is worse: Death or exile? Oblivion or rootlessness?

We are finally set free, and the world instead turns inward.

Time zips by with the speed of a thumb on a touchscreen. A smiling family dancing in unison to a Top 40 song. A mother pleading for formula to feed her daughter. Here are five things married people do. Here are five vegetables to plant in your backyard garden. Here are five steps to financial health. A sea of tents amid the quad I used to cross on my way to the library. The police are called. The protesters are beaten, locked away, doxxed, deported. "This is not about free speech. This is about people that don't have a right to be in the United States." We shiver with recognition.

We know that a house is made of bricks and mortar and can collapse, but every day I dream of a little bungalow just big enough for my love and me, a set of pots to make him dinner, and a garden to catch the sun—that no one can take away from us. Once, we brought a sick bird inside and it flew away the next morning, healed by safety.

What happens to fear without four walls to keep it in? I know. We've always known, it's just that no one has believed us.

—California, 2025

FREEDOM

I arrive in Johannesburg, South Africa, on December 2, 2013. My father will join me in two weeks, with my brother to follow a week later. In one month, we will unveil my mother's headstone in the township where she grew up, one year after her death. Weeks before my arrival, a report detailing the unlawful expenditure of taxpayer money in the form of $20 million of "security improvements" to President Jacob Zuma's lavish compound is leaked to the press. Nine years ago, the country's first all-race elections were held and South Africa finally regained its freedom from apartheid rule.

Pennsylvania this time of year is frigid and snow-kissed, and even though I am anxious about what will await me on this trip, I am thankful for the warm South African weather and all the charms that come along with it. In South African culture, the headstone unveiling traditionally resembles a funeral in scope, usually consisting of a service at the graveyard and a repast afterward.

As Americans, my father, brother, and I are stumbling into this ritual somewhat blindly, leaving the details to my type-A older cousin, Annemarie. The ceremony will take place on Christmas Day, followed by a traditional lunch. After that, my adult cousins and I will board a plane to much warmer Cape Town on the southern coast, where many of Johannesburg's residents spend the festive season.

These two weeks mark the first time I have been in this country alone. Throughout most of my life, my family and I have spent summers here visiting my relatives, but this is the first time I've crossed the ocean by myself, the first time I've been left solely in charge of planning which sights to see, which friends to visit. For the first time, I will have complete control over my own travel. My mother was, for much of our twenty-seven years together, an incredibly fearful person. The 1990s and early 2000s were violent years in South Africa, and as children, our movements were tightly controlled. This is the first time I will experience some freedom on my own, and it doesn't escape me that it has come at the cost of my mother's life, and also—perhaps because of this fact—I am both scared and excited.

My mother was named Dorothy, called "Dotty" for short. Born in 1957, she was the second youngest of five children from a middle-class coloured—or mixed-race—family from Johannesburg's western suburbs, where they were placed after being removed from the neighborhood of Jeppe by the Group Areas Act, the legislation enforcing racial segregation during apartheid.

My mother was the first one in her family to attend college. She was the first non-white student to move into her college dormitory. She became involved in the anti-apartheid struggle there, against the wishes of my grandparents. In 1976, when she was nineteen, the Soweto Uprising occurred, and my grandfather, who worked as an undertaker, buried the bodies of murdered schoolchildren from the nearby black township.

She met my father in Botswana in the eighties, while she was smuggling banned literature back into South Africa. My father was volunteering in the country, a visitor from his US college. After a brief courtship, my mother moved to the States, where they settled in Philadelphia and she entered graduate school.

Growing up in the 1990s and early 2000s, I would hear her relay the wrenching events of her workday as a public school teacher in inner-city Philadelphia every day, unaware of how she had heard similar stories from her father as a child—stories of children who were neglected and sometimes abused by parents who were themselves products of a broken system. I didn't understand where her commitment to these children came from, why she kept at it through the challenges and the frustration. I was too young to understand the concept of injustice as it related to her work.

If she once craved freedom in her youth, she grew to fear it in her later years. Whenever I hear stories of my mother's past, the woman she was in her younger years seems unrecognizable to me. America reshaped her. Faced with the choice of assimilation or resistance, she chose the former. Her accent dulled, especially in the company of Americans. She became fascinated with

American pop culture. Like many black Americans, her desire for conformity took the form of striving, which she channeled into her children. She kept a tight leash on us—me especially. I was just as rebellious as she was when she was younger, and therefore, we were constantly at odds.

In 2010, at fifty-three, she was diagnosed with late-stage multiple myeloma, a cancer of the white blood cells that normally afflicts the elderly. She kept working, became closer than ever to her South African family. Her mother died ten years before her diagnosis; after her death, my mother became the family's unofficial matriarch. She was always outspoken and personable, and the role suited her naturally. Even from a distance, she was entrenched in gossip, a confidante for my young cousins and aunts and uncles alike. When she became sick, several of them traveled to America, many for the first time, to help us take care of her and—though they wouldn't admit it then—to say goodbye.

After I was long gone from her house and living in New York City, cancer made her confront death and the fears that came along with it. We got along better than we ever had, started to finally accept each other's flaws and appreciate each other as people. We became friends. And then, just as soon, she was gone.

I stay with my aunt Avril, who lives in an old mansion on a large property in the wealthy northern suburbs of Johannesburg. I remember when they first moved in, what a source of pride it was for her and our entire family. It was bought by her ex-husband, a country boy made good who runs a property development business. Now divorced, he lives only a few miles away and still visits her home for dinner. Avril was my mom's closest sister, with her independent streak and bawdy sense of humor. She tells loud, dirty jokes in mixed company, to which listeners exclaim "Oh, Avie!" with mock exasperation. She has all of my mother's charms and few of her hang-ups.

"I'm not over it," she tells me now, in regard to her sister's death, and she is so open that I can see all the broken parts inside her.

On my second day, still jet-lagged, I wake up late, around 11 a.m. On my way to the kitchen, Avie stops me in the hallway. I can tell by the way she pauses that something has happened. *I can't take more bad news*, I think to myself.

She tells me that Nelson Mandela died early in the morning, just a few neighborhoods over, in another upscale enclave called Houghton. She's been up watching the news for hours, she says.

My cousins and I made plans earlier to gather at my cousin Kim's house in Fourways. It was supposed to be our first night out together. Instead, we order in Chinese food and drink Kim's good bottles of red wine. They talk about Mandela's death, what they think it will mean for the country's future.

Stacey tells me about one of her coworkers, a black girl a few years younger than her, who dismissed the fuss their office was making. "So, he died?" she huffed, and went on about her day. We all cluck and roll our eyes, because we remember how things were before. We all live in the shadow of our parents' apartheid stories. The younger generation—the so-called Born Frees, or those born after independence—are not the same. Stacey's boyfriend is white. Stacey has always been hard-nosed, quick-tempered, but he has softened her in the way that love does.

After a couple more glasses of wine, Stacey looks at me and says with a soft, tipsy smile, "I keep thinking, how lucky it is that your mom gets to meet Mandela in heaven."

The mood in the city is one of restrained mourning. Mandela's name comes up often in conversation; the radios play a constant stream of downtempo ballads and gospel songs and, between commercial breaks, prerecorded tributes, always with a conspicuous plug for the station, reminding us who sponsored this *deeply* emotional shared experience. The mood is not one strictly of sadness. The mourning is respectful, laced with celebration, jubilation even. I see it in the South African flags my family members place outside their houses, in the people who chant and sing revolutionary songs outside Mandela's home; in the tones of admiration that punctuate any discussion of him. The mix of tragedy and pride, of ululating and flag waving, hearkens directly back to independence in 1994. That day, my parents took me out of school early so that I could stand beside my mother in the Philadelphia Civic Center as she cast her first vote for Mandela's ANC Party.

They announce that there will be a public memorial service at FNB Stadium in Soweto. Dozens of heads of state will be in attendance and the entire city will be completely devoted to it over the next week. I need to go, I tell my family. As large as the service is expected to be, it's on a Tuesday and the government does not declare a holiday, so all of my family goes to work. I try to organize a ride with family friends, friends of friends; I reach out to anyone who says they may be going.

The roads around the stadium will be closed, and public transportation will be made freely available to and from the site. A new system of express buses and commuter trains is in place, built to support the 2010 World Cup. Before then, transportation was highly dangerous and unreliable. The private minibuses, called taxis, and PUTCO buses that service most of the black population are the frequent cause of fatal highway crashes.

My family, though, still lives in the past. They have not yet caught up to the reality that, even though things are still dangerous, they are better today. Like many, their trauma of years ago, above all else, determines their reality. They bristle when I tell them I want to go. On the morning of the memorial, all of my leads have gone nowhere, and I resign myself to watching the service on TV at my grandfather's house.

When I arrive, my cousin Terri is on her way to work. Her family lives in an apartment that adjoins my grandparents' house in the back. Terri is too cool for my family's hometown: a budding hipster and graphic designer who reminds me of myself at twenty-three. Weekends, she hops warehouse parties and gallery openings in Maboneng, the newly redeveloped arts neighborhood in Joburg's Central Business District, a place that not long ago was a no-man's-land for the middle and working classes. She encourages me to go by myself, tells me her friends are at the stadium already and they can save me a seat.

Terri and her sisters, Kim and Stacey, joke that because of apartheid, they're all different races. Kim, the eldest, is coloured, because she spent most of her life segregated with other coloureds. Stacey, the middle sister, is white, because she came of age when coloureds and whites were just starting to mix; and Terri, the youngest, is black. The "coloured" moniker is an invention of apartheid, created to separate mixed-race people from blacks and pit them against one another. But Terri has cast off those divisions. Most of her friends are black. She is also like me on this account, because even though I could claim multiraciality, I've always called myself black. There is no such category as "coloured" in the United States, and according to the one-drop rule, that's what I am, and I've never resisted it, have always felt proud to be black. It's one of the things my cousins find most foreign about me.

My uncle drives me to an express bus stop nearby. He speaks to another coloured man and his wife and daughter. He introduces us. He's asked the man to watch out for me on the way over. Right after my uncle bids me farewell and heads to work, the man taps me on the shoulder. The small pocket on my backpack is open, revealing my keys and cell phone. I smile, try to laugh it off, but I know I've exposed myself as a hapless tourist. I try to look more serious.

As the bus winds toward Soweto, it becomes increasingly full of black passengers. After our penultimate stop, the woman next to me shouts a note and the entire bus erupts in song. We ride that way, buoyed by music, up to the stadium hill.

I walk with my fellow passengers and find Terri's friends

quickly. They are all black, stylish like her, friendly, and totally unequipped for the rain. It is one of the coldest days since I've been here, and it pours relentlessly. We sit shivering under two umbrellas shared among the six of us. Because of the weather and because people are at work, the stadium never fills as it's supposed to. Still, the service is stately and jubilant. People wear the yellow, green, and black of the ANC. They drape themselves in multicolored South African flags. Many of them are wearing trash bags to shield themselves from the rain, some have wrapped their boots in plastic shopping bags. They file into the stadium chanting, and when President Zuma is introduced onstage, they boo him gleefully. They cheer Thabo Mbeki, Mandela's successor, who has become a hero again after leaving office in disgrace, carried out on a wave of populist fervor. Robert Mugabe also receives a round of applause, as does Barack Obama.

This is the first time I've gone anywhere in South Africa completely on my own, and I stop to appreciate the moment. I'm independent to a fault, I hate restrictions, and I buckle when anyone tries to control me. Here, in this unfamiliar place filled with strangers, I feel blissful. I'm in awe of the size of the stadium, the swelling chants, the euphoria, and the feeling that I am part of something bigger than any of us.

Annemarie's husband is a successful lawyer with a practice in town. Whenever we're out in public, someone will come up to him and ask for advice. I spend a few nights in their home, an elegant stucco structure with huge walls of windows that look onto green hills and orange Johannesburg sunsets. They built it a couple of years ago at the top of a hill in a neighborhood with a view onto the scenic hills of Johannesburg's northern suburbs. Their house is positioned directly across from a nature reserve, giving them one of the best unobstructed views of the surrounding landscape with lush jacaranda trees and stately manicured lawns.

One day, as we're pulling out of the driveway, we notice police vehicles across the street at the reserve. A section of the gate is lying flat on the ground, looking like a gap-toothed smile. Before the fallen gate are a squadron of police and private security cars. The officers are dressed in full Kevlar, guns at the ready, gazing into the reserve. Inside, there are more officers running over the hills.

Annemarie's two young children are in the car with us. They grow excited at the flashing lights; they giggle and squirm when Annemarie pulls up next to a squad car, lowers the window, and asks the officer what's happened.

He tells us there was a home invasion a few blocks over, on the same street that my aunt Veronica lives on. One of the homeowners was shot as well as one of the robbers. The rest of the suspects are still on the loose.

As we pull away, Annemarie's son giddily imitates a police officer with his gun, holding his fingers up to his sister's face. He pulls the trigger and they both explode in delight. Annemarie tells me about the time she heard gunshots when she was standing in her bathroom. She dropped instinctively to the floor and stayed there until her husband came home. Her children laugh uproariously at the story, saying, "Mom, you're so paranoid!" I urge Annemarie to drive faster.

Later that night, when we're returning to the house to sleep, I ask Annemarie if she is scared. She tells me she is very security-conscious. She talks about the alarms and the motion-detector beams in the yard. She never actually answers my question.

Crime ballooned around the 1980s and 1990s, a consequence of the country's struggle for freedom—a reason cited by apartheid sympathizers for why things were better "back in those days." My family's conservatism has always chafed, and I certainly don't tell them that when it comes down to it, I side with the so-called criminals over them. How could I feel any other way when faced with miles upon miles of informal settlements housing the country's blacks and coloureds? I recognize it as a postcolonial hangover, a feature of the country's massive unemployment and politicians' broken promises. I hate how it shapes every day of my life here. I am not just resigned to this violence, I know it is deserved. Part of me thinks that I deserve it, too.

I barely sleep that night. I go to the window every hour or so to gaze across their yard at the nature reserve. The section of gate is still down, and every once in a while a security van passes, lights whirling, throwing yellow onto the yard and into the hills around us.

My cousins and I party almost every night. My mother never would have let us behave in this way, but no one else seems to care. I don't remember my grief when we are drunk and the car is speeding down the highway. We drive with the windows down and blast music, the smoke from my cousins' cigarettes flooding my face. I sit in the back seat, feeling the warm rush of South African air, feeling happy to be alive. So we drink and play roulette with our vehicle. My mother continues to be dead. I drink until there are no discrete words echoing in my head, only the loud thumping of the radio: a thick veil of sadness.

On the day of the unveiling, Christmas Day, my brother, father, and I wake early in the morning for church. We dress solemnly in our separate rooms. I opt for a bright purple kimono I bought in downtown Johannesburg instead of the black dress that I first wore to my mother's funeral.

Before I head out the door I swallow a Lorazepam—a low-dose prescription I have for flying—as Annemarie instructed me last night. I'm exhausted and hungover when I wake up, and the Lorazepam makes it almost impossible for me to stay awake. I feel like I am wrapped in cotton all day, comfortable and insulated from everything around me.

After church, we regroup at my grandfather's house and then drive to the graveyard together. There is a tent set up around the plot where my grandmother is buried, a few plastic chairs underneath. Fittingly, it is raining and cold, the worst weather since the Mandela memorial. A new stone stands next to my grandmother's, covered in black cloth. My brother and I take a seat just in front of it. My father reads a Bible verse. They remove the cloth and there is my mother's name. As many times as I've seen it on funeral programs and obituaries, I'm always jarred to be confronted with it in this context. It is the worst part, the moment my grief hits me the hardest, when I have to remind myself that my mother is dead. My mother is dead.

Thanks to the pill, I don't cry as much as I thought I would or had feared. I float through the ceremony, hugging the twenty or so relatives assembled at the grave, and I doze off in the car on the way back to Avie's house. I fall asleep in my room until lunch, which I eat outside by the pool with my cousins, wearing tissue-paper crowns from our Christmas crackers. We pack what's remaining to be packed and then we're driven to the airport.

It is our second-to-last night in Cape Town, after which I will return to Johannesburg for two more days, and then my father and I will leave on a plane back to Philadelphia. I meet my family friend, Celeste, and we decide it will be good to let off some steam, just the two of us. Plus, we have a lot to talk about.

Celeste chooses a nightclub nearby in the neighborhood of Greenpoint that is nicely outfitted but surprisingly small. It feels intimate and deceptively friendly. Celeste and I are in our element. We sit next to a massive VIP area that takes up half of the club, outfitted with couches and tables. Early in the night, a group of young men in collared shirts shake bottles of Moët and spray them around the room, rap video style. The waitresses wipe the tables after them. When some of it sprays on me, I scream at them playfully. One of the men looks at me and smiles, then hands me an entire bottle as an apology. I've always been amused by the stereotypes of African poverty for how incomplete they are. Africa is not a monolith but a land of extremes: The poor do not exist without the rich.

Celeste is a lawyer, the first in either of our families. She grew up in a house next to my grandparents' in Bosmont and has been close with my family all our lives. She's survived an onslaught of difficulties—the death of her best friend in grade school, a hijacking a few years ago, instability in her family—that have made her interesting and wise. She is the person I'm closest to in South Africa, and I often think about what things would be like if we lived in the same country. She wonders this, too, and regularly floats the idea of moving to the States, but it never happens. She is very beautiful. She has a square jaw and dainty features, plus an air of gravity and wisdom—born of a hard life—that is magnetic.

We let some men buy us drinks and accept none of their advances. I have a boyfriend at home, who I will leave shortly after I return from this trip, and Celeste is still going through breakup trauma from her five-year relationship ending. We laugh once they've exited our orbit and swap stories of tacky clothes and bad breath.

At the end of the night, as the club starts to empty, we wander over to the VIP section. We dance on the couches with girls who must be models, they are so thin and beautiful. We cross paths with a caramel-skinned man with a big paunch. He is dressed flamboyantly, in designer sunglasses, with big rings on his fingers. He is effeminate and effusively friendly. I sense no romantic attraction and there is none whatsoever on my end, even though he shows instant interest in us.

He tells us his name is Maurice. Celeste tells him she used to live in Australia with her boyfriend, and he says he has an office there. When I tell him I lived in New York, he tells us of his apartment on the Upper East Side. He doesn't respond directly when we ask him what he does for a living.

When the lights come back on, he stays put while the rest of the revelers file out and the black-uniformed crew comes in to clean up the mess. The staff is attentive to him and, for some reason, doesn't ask him to leave. Instead, he orders us more drinks and they bring them to us with a smile.

He tells us that he's staying downtown in the Westin. Celeste elbows me excitedly as he tells us about his trips around the world, shows us a video taken up-close of Obama behind the scenes at Mandela's memorial. I lie down on the banquette because the room is spinning. I tell Celeste I think I should go home, but she doesn't hear me. She pulls me off the banquette and we follow him into a cab.

The staff at the Westin is also attentive to him. He leads us up to a nicely equipped room that is strewn with luxury goods—a Tom Ford watch here, Gucci shoes there. The room continues to spin and I get into the lone king bed, tuck myself under the covers. He sits in a chair by the window and Celeste dances excitedly between us, blissfully drunk. I haven't seen her this carefree in so long. It makes me deeply happy, as even through my haze I can recognize that.

There is a large-screen plasma opposite the bed tuned to

CNN, and as the sun rises our conversation thins, becomes dull, and Celeste announces she's leaving to have a cigarette.

The door barely clicks closed and things happen in a seeming instant. I don't remember him walking over to the bed. I am on my feet, in his arms, and his tongue is in my mouth, aggressive, hungry. I can feel his teeth on my tongue. He tries to pull my dress over my head. He doesn't ask if I want to do any of this, never pauses to assess my willingness. The fact that I am too drunk to stand on my own is ignored—nay, discarded.

"Wait," I manage to say, as carefully as my drunkenness will allow. I don't say "stop," I say "wait," which is gentler, because I don't want to risk how he might react if I reject him. I don't need to think through these actions; my body performs them automatically, as a means of survival. As his hands find my breasts I wonder how far I will have to go to escape without violence. My mind makes a quick calculation: If he's capable of this, he's capable of much worse. I shut down—my eyes close, my mind stops protesting—in preparation for what is about to happen.

Then the door opens and Celeste reenters the room, accompanied by a man from the desk. When he hears them, Maurice darts back over to his chair. Celeste couldn't remember the room number, and the front desk wouldn't give it to her (hotel policy), but they would escort her back.

Adrenaline coursing, I stumble out of bed and whisper to Celeste that it's time to leave. She's still giddy, excited by the big hotel room and its mysterious occupant; it takes her a while to grasp my urgency. When she does, we run out of the room without a goodbye, and in the lobby the staff hails us a cab.

On the ride home, I tell her what happened. She tells me that the people at the desk told her the man's name wasn't Maurice. They wouldn't tell her what his real name was, but it wasn't that.

We cry together in the back of the cab, and she holds me. When we get back to the house, the sun is blazing brightly and the rest of the cousins are still fast asleep. Celeste and I decide not to tell them; it's too much, this latest drama, and they'll only blame us for it. We're women, we shouldn't have gone out by ourselves and gotten so drunk. Celeste shouldn't have left me alone with a strange man. We know that none of them will place the appropriate blame with the person who deserves it.

The sun is rising on another ludicrously beautiful day in Cape Town; we see the water, and all the beautiful buildings that dot the coastline. I say nothing. It's easier to carry this thing on our own.

Before long, it is my last day in South Africa. I have Annemarie take me to Soweto, which is a thirty-minute drive from my grandparents' house. We drive to Vilakazi Street, to the modest Mandela family home that has been turned into a museum. Vendors peddling screen-printed shirts bearing the departed leader's face line the blocks leading to the house. We barter with them for souvenirs, and my cousin chides them, "I'm from here, don't try to take my money!" She tells them she knows they've made a killing since he died. They are sheepish, smiling in return, and stop short of saying that this hero's death has been good for business. *Good for them*, I think.

Mandela's home is an old matchbox, identical to the many hundreds of modest four-room brick houses built by the government to house poor, mostly black residents. Many more were supposed to be built, enough to house all the people who need them, but it never happened. Instead, more mansions are built and the informal settlements grow.

Mandela's house is tiny on the inside and decorated with awards and curios from all over the world, including some from Pennsylvania. Soweto looks very different from how it's pictured in photos from Mandela's days—many of the houses have been expanded with extra floors and wings, with gaudy security fencing and fancy cars in the driveway.

Annemarie tells me that, even though she grew up only thirty minutes away, this is her first time in Soweto. This is not uncommon for coloured people of her age, for whom Soweto will always be synonymous with battle. Annemarie was a young child when the Uprising happened, not much younger than the students who were shot at and killed that day. Through the 1980s, Soweto was ground zero for anti-apartheid political violence, with frequent armed skirmishes taking place in the streets. For them, the divisions of apartheid remain alive as ever. She thanks me, laughing, for coming all the way from America to bring her here.

Annemarie was raised by my grandparents, which in effect made her and my mother sisters. They were extremely close, and as a result, Annemarie is something of an aunt to me. She tells me that my mother used to hang here all the time back when she was in college.

"She'd come on a Friday, drink till she fell off her chair in one of the shebeens, and then call us to come get her." Annemarie mocks holding an invisible phone to her ear, imitating my mother. "We're getting raided!" she yells into her finger, and we fall out laughing.

Soon, my mind goes back to what happened to me in the hotel room. Ever since it happened, I have been fighting off the thought of it constantly. I think how angry our families would be at Celeste and me if they knew. I think that the chances that the same thing, or worse, happened to my mother years ago, seem very high. I wonder, if we'd had more years together, if she would have told me.

In this moment, I can see my mother as a young woman. I can see her wandering the dusty red streets of Soweto, ducking in and out of houses, chatting with the people in her confident way. In my mind's eye, she looks just like me. She is curious, intelligent, and trailed by the threat of danger. For most of my life, my mother was the authoritarian, my foil. But today I see her as another version of me, and I wonder why it has taken me so long to realize that.

It will take me years to face what happened to me that night in Cape Town. I will become scared to return. But I will never stop loving these people, this land, the life that so many are able to live here thanks to what happened in these streets, the blood shed over so many years.

I think about the interminable nature of struggle, how oppression recedes and returns, how it must be fought constantly.

CHASING ROBBIE

Crime is a phenomenon of organized social life, and is the open rebellion of an individual against his social environment.

—W. E. B. Du Bois, *The Philadelphia Negro*

The native town, the Negro village, the medina, the reservation, is a place of ill fame, peopled by men of evil repute. They are born there, it matters little where or how; they die there, it matters not where, nor how.

—Frantz Fanon, *The Wretched of the Earth*

Driving north from Delaware into Chester, Pennsylvania, depending on which day you are here, you may notice an unpleasant smell. Upon crossing the southern border into the city, you are immediately greeted by the Covanta incinerator plant, which processes waste from Pennsylvania, New Jersey, and Maryland. Chester's profusion of garbage dumps, incinerators, and medical-waste disposal sites make it one of the most notorious sites of environmental racism in the United States. Rows of conjoined brick homes are strewn with debris, every few doors and windows are boarded up or hollowed out. Interstate 95, the Eastern Seaboard's main thoroughfare, carelessly bisects the length of the city, and driving east to west you will see cars whizzing at top speed mere feet away from these houses, separated by nothing but a chain-link fence.

The landscape becomes sparser as you wind up Providence Road through Widener University, then cross Ridley Creek and

Houston Park, where there suddenly appear single-family homes with wide lawns, then a stretch of tidy shopping centers with a gas station, a bike shop, and a gourmet market. Traffic slows to a crawl as you reach a canopy of verdant trees and generous stone-fronted houses. You have reached Swarthmore, population 6,500—home to Swarthmore College, among the nation's most prestigious—and one of the best places to live in Pennsylvania. You can feel the calm and exclusivity as you wind along the near-empty, tree-lined streets and pass impossibly graceful Tudors and Victorians with yard signs touting local Democratic candidates, ABORTION IS HEALTHCARE, and IN THIS HOUSE WE BELIEVE . . . You will feel you've found your way into some liberal suburban paradise, a lifetime away from your starting point in Chester—but in reality it's only been a ten-minute drive.

This was roughly the course charted by Robert Allen Payne. Robbie, as I knew him, was one of the first students I met when I arrived in Swarthmore. He was known as a jokester, his last name occasioned a sometimes nickname for the way he used to tease his classmates. I was a frequent target for one reason or another, but I rarely minded. He was a constant source of levity and at times vexation. In a town where I felt nothing but alienation, he was an island of familiarity, like a brother or a cousin—at once a foil and a mirror.

At Swarthmore-Rutledge School, I was one of three black students in my year and the only black girl. I'd arrived halfway through third grade and found myself met with deep culture shock. I learned quickly that black families like mine—upwardly mobile, with both parents in the home—were a rarity in this community. One black boy came from a public housing community in Woodlyn, Pennsylvania. The other was Robbie. We were drawn together by fate. I don't know what I would have done without him.

Robbie was lighthearted, always with a huge smile that swallowed his whole face. He preferred not to dip into the darker aspects of his childhood with myself and my classmates, though we knew they were there. Only the outlines of his story were known. He had come to Swarthmore from Chester when he was young. Like many other black children we knew, his parents struggled and were unable to take care of him. Nevertheless, he remained close to his family there and in Philadelphia. In his teenage years, he lost his younger sister in a car accident. He was close to his aunt Dorris and uncle Butch, who raised him in Swarthmore. He seemed to bear it all extremely well, never letting on about the pain the situation must have caused him, at least in public.

At our high school, Strath Haven, Robbie flourished. He grew up surrounded by a close-knit community in the Historically Black Neighborhood of Swarthmore (HBNS), including an extended family who had lived there for generations. He had legions of friends of all races and stripes. He excelled in track and field, football, and basketball. Upon graduation, he earned a basketball scholarship to Lackawanna College. He was popular, handsome, and universally liked.

Our paths started to diverge in middle school, when I formed bonds with the alternative, bookish crowd I found in my honors classes, art classes, and quiz bowl team. Sometime around high school, we became strangers, separated by artificial but vital social strata. He was still my brother, and when I looked at him, I saw layers of history and familiarity, and what I would later recognize as love. I was too young to know how to express that, and in our distancing, I lost some part of me.

In 2009, seemingly out of nowhere, Robbie started sending me messages on Facebook. He was upbeat, his normal jokester self.

"heyy . . . where are you these days?" he asked.

As I filled him in on the details of my life, I felt the distance between us begin to narrow. I was living in Brooklyn and working at a publishing house while writing on the side. I told him about my plans to attend grad school, to move apartments, to visit my family in Philadelphia. He told me that he'd finished college and had moved back home. He'd planned to go to law school and he was studying hard for his LSATs. He told me about the books he was reading. He seemed genuinely interested in what I was doing.

"We should get together before you go back," he wrote.

I didn't know how to relate to him: as a friend, a brother, or something else? We never did see each other. Perhaps he felt the same.

On July 4, 2016, Robbie was celebrating at the annual block party in his Swarthmore neighborhood. They'd set up tables and chairs at the corner of Brighton and Bowdoin Avenues like they had every year, the celebration a tradition for generations of black Swarthmoreans. After reveling with friends and family, he left the party around 4:30 p.m. and drove back to Chester to pick up a friend. While his car idled outside her home at Third and Kerlin Streets, he was approached by an unknown shooter who opened fire with a high-powered assault rifle similar to an AK-47. In total, Robbie suffered twenty-three entry wounds. His friend exited her house, found him, and called 911. Police arrived on the scene, found him unresponsive, and declared him dead.

On July 5, I woke up to a text from my brother, Mark, addressed to my father and me. I had been living in Los Angeles for a few short months and Mark was in New Jersey, where he still saw his high school friends regularly. He's always been connected to that place in a way that I never was. I often envy the facility with which he relates to the people we grew up with. I lost touch with nearly everyone from there aside from a couple of friends.

He delivered the news in his typical blunt manner. Robbie got shot. Robbie was dead. He sent a link to a local news story that identified a man killed in Chester, Pennsylvania. I read each word of the text individually, then the news article, but for many moments they didn't add up. I hadn't spoken to Robbie in a few years, but his name called up that old familiarity, his round, burnt-sugar face, memories of my childhood. And then the words—shot to death in his vehicle. Reality intruded like a sharp knife.

At the time of Robbie's death, shootings were a common story in Chester. The same year, *The Philadelphia Inquirer* found that the Chester Police had closed only about one-third of the city's 323 homicides since 2000—roughly half the national average and one of the lowest rates in the country. The reasons for this failure:

high crime and lack of resources to properly investigate, combined with the community's lack of trust in law enforcement. "The vast majority of homicides, we have a real good idea who did it," Joe Ryan, chief of Delaware County's Criminal Investigation Division, told *The Philadelphia Inquirer* in 2016. In recent years, interventions in Chester, similar to those enacted in nearby Trenton, New Jersey, have produced a turnaround in these numbers. Chester Partnership for Safe Neighborhoods (CPSN)—a collaboration between public agencies, community groups, and law enforcement—lowered the gun homicide rate 72 percent from 2019 to 2024 and raised the homicide clearance rate to 61 percent. Even given these changes, Chester's homicide rate remains high compared to the rest of the United States, and sadly, these improvements have come too late for people like Robbie.

A few witnesses gathered in the aftermath of Robbie's shooting near the intersection of Third and Kerlin Streets. None of them, the police said, would cooperate with the investigation. Robbie's friend who found him initially gave a statement to police but eventually stopped talking. The story has been revisited by the local press nearly every year since his murder, but to this day there have been no developments. I have heard others speak with confidence about who murdered Robbie, with little expectation that this person will be charged or prosecuted. It seems clear from these accounts that Robbie was not the intended target. But the specifics of what happened to him are not the realm of this essay—I will leave that to another writer. In any case, I do not expect such details alone to provide justice or closure. I know that victimhood is expansive, that perpetrators are almost always victims themselves, a fact unaccounted for in our so-called justice system. Justice is best sought elsewhere, and closure usually finds you when you stop looking for it.

Robbie was portrayed in the press as a devoted teacher who moved back to his hometown to serve his community at Chester High School. His many friends, all of whom he called his "best friend," turned out in the hundreds for his memorial service, which I was unable to fly back to Pennsylvania in time for. I learned that he had a baby on the way at the time he was murdered.

As the years passed, the shock of his murder slowly waned, but its brutality continues to unsettle me. With every news article, I relive the senselessness of it and its incongruousness to the nature of its victim. I'm haunted by the thought of Robbie, alone in his final moments. In my grief, I write him a letter. "I wish I had something more elegant to say, but you did not deserve this." His death hangs open, a question mark. My mind casts about for answers.

The threat of violence has always floated on the periphery of my consciousness, quietly molding my thoughts and shaping my life. South Africa during the late 1980s and 1990s, where my mother's family lived and we spent months at a time, was the most potent example, when the unrest of the independence years spawned massive waves of interpersonal violence. There, we lived in constant fear of carjackings, assaults, and home invasions. Everyone had a story to tell about a neighbor who was awoken by an intruder and shot or a friend held up at a stoplight. When I was around ten years old, a neighbor streamed into my grandmother's kitchen one night, his white undershirt slashed, revealing torn red flesh underneath. I watched my grandmother clean his wounds with water from the large white bowl she used to make our Sunday dinners. When robbers accosted my uncle as he drove toward his gate, they abducted him at gunpoint to a field, and he narrowly escaped, returning to his home in the morning.

To the extent these events molded me, as an American, and as a coloured person from a middle-class family, I was insulated from them. Early on, I learned that one's proximity to violence is determined by privilege. The poorer, the blacker, the more disabled you are, the more mortality presents in your daily life.

In America, we spent most of our time as a family between black neighborhoods in Jamaica, Queens; Philadelphia; and Washington, DC, where our family and friends lived, all of which were experiencing spikes in violent crime. We would sometimes hear gunshots late at night, and we were kept on a short leash during the day. We couldn't go anywhere without our parents' permission, and in certain places we weren't allowed outdoors at all. Like all black children, we were given constant, heavy warnings about the police. We were especially vulnerable, our parents reminded us, and danger was everywhere.

Everywhere but where we lived, that was. To my peers in Swarthmore, death was aberrant, allowing them to belt out violent rap lyrics and fantasize about gun violence from the comfort of their luxury cars and the safety of their cul-de-sacs. In Swarthmore, there was no chance of anything happening to us. My mother locked all the windows and set the security alarm every night. Swarthmore ensconced us in safety, a protective bubble that would follow me throughout my life: from a good high school to a good college, then to a good job that set us up in similarly safe towns, with friends who were also shielded from violence. Swarthmore meant we'd grow up living lives unlike those of my mother's students in the inner city and unlike the lives our parents lived in their youths. In South Africa, our safety was self-reinforcing: Our aunts, uncles, and even our cousins shielded us from the vagaries of life there, protected us because we were sheltered, special children. This was the promise of Swarthmore, for which black families like ours were willing to sacrifice almost everything.

I arrived in Swarthmore from the north, from a mostly black suburb called Yeadon just on the other side of Philadelphia's western border. My memories of Yeadon are happy; we were part of a community of young black families whose futures looked bright. Jasmine, my best friend since we were three years old, lived only a few blocks away. Her father and my parents all graduated from the University of Pennsylvania, and our families are lifelong friends; we remain in touch to this day. We lived in a twin house with a big front porch, a backyard where we planted marigolds and I splashed in a plastic wading pool on hot summer days. We learned to ride bikes in the alleyway behind my house, and we'd pick mulberries off our neighbor's bush when they ripened in the spring.

There were dark things that happened there, too. One day, we received news that a friend's mother had been murdered in her home blocks away from ours; my friend and her sister discovered her body in the vestibule of their white-columned home upon returning from school. There was the shooting in the apartment complex across the street from our house. And one evening we returned home to find our basement window busted out and our belongings missing. Soon after we found out that the crime was committed by a troubled neighborhood boy, my parents decided that we would leave.

Yeadon's mostly black school district, William Penn, is one of the lowest-performing in the state, so while we lived there, my parents sent us to a nearby private Quaker school instead. The decision to move came as the tuition became too onerous, and they swapped private school fees for higher property taxes in the Wallingford-Swarthmore School District, one of the best in the state. They found a modest split-level home on the outskirts of Swarthmore. It was only a twenty-minute drive away from Yeadon in the southern part of the same county, Delaware.

Our childhood in Swarthmore looked idyllic. We played in the streets until dark and roamed free in the college campus's nationally recognized arboretum. On snow days in elementary school, we sledded down the hill in front of Parrish Hall; in high school, we held bonfires in the woods that surrounded Crum Creek. I had what has become increasingly rare these days: an excellent public education. Save for certain factors, I could have called the entire experience happy.

The area now known as Swarthmore was granted by William

Penn in the early 1600s to the Quakers, who would settle and occupy the rural countryside for the proceeding centuries. In the early nineteenth century it became known as Westdale, in honor of the famous painter Benjamin West, born there in 1738. In 1864, the Hicksite branch of the Society of Friends founded Swarthmore College to educate their children. The college, along with a rail line that connected it to Philadelphia in 1854, began the process of development from rural countryside to suburban commuter town. Swarthmore was incorporated as a borough—a form of municipal government in Pennsylvania equivalent to a town elsewhere—in 1893. Today, Swarthmore's population numbers 6,543. The median household income hovers around $147,000 per year, nearly twice the median income of households in Pennsylvania, while its poverty ratio is roughly one-quarter the average in Pennsylvania. Swarthmore's population is 74 percent white, 6 percent black, 7 percent Hispanic or Latino, and 11 percent Asian.

Despite its reputation as a liberal haven, Swarthmore's racial history is typical for a northern small town. The borough remained segregated until the 1960s, when black residents were allowed to buy in a designated area now named the HBNS. A series of racist terror incidents, including arsons and cross burnings, were committed against families that attempted to integrate in the 1950s and 1960s. In 1958, the white Yarrow family attempted to sell their house to a black family, in a deliberate attempt at desegregation. In response, the Swarthmore Friends Meeting sent a letter to the Yarrows: "We feel that you are deliberately depreciating the value of your neighbors' real estate when you sell your home to colored people. . . . [We] beg you to reconsider your plan . . . and to withdraw from your apparent position of discrimination against white buyers." Around the same time, in nearby Rutledge, a house burned down the night before the family of George T. Raymond, president of the NAACP in Chester, was scheduled to move in. The Swarthmore Friends Society remained conflicted on the issue of segregation through this time, as it struggled for years to find consensus on a public statement in support of integration that was finally made official in 1961. Swarthmore has resisted affordable and dense housing developments to this day, and with gentrification taking hold, it remains a wealthy, mostly white enclave where black residents are still, for the large part, confined to the same neighborhoods they were when segregation was law.

My parents made no secret of the fact that we'd settled there exclusively for the schools, and partly as a result, we held the place at arm's length, never fully integrating. But that distancing also came from the knowledge that something ugly lay below the surface. We were middle class, my parents were well educated and owned our home, and we were light complexioned—not like those "other" black people, we were sometimes told—so we didn't suffer the worst outright instances of racism. But the place pushed back against us in different ways.

Robbie's cousin Ray is a spitting image of Robbie, even all these years later. He texts me photos of his children, and I see the resemblance that they share with Robbie's son, Nasir. Nasir is seven by now, but in the pictures he's still an infant, with Robbie's bright eyes, round nose, and devilish smile in miniature. Always together, Ray and Robbie cut handsome figures in our high school days. I remember Ray fondly. He would stop to chat with me, making me forget for one small moment my place at the bottom of the high school social pyramid. Ray was four years ahead of us, so those moments, however fond, were brief. He grew up in Swarthmore on a street surrounded by his relatives, where one of his ancestors built six of the conjoined houses on Kenyon Avenue in the Historically Black Neighborhood. His roots there were deep, and he speaks of them with immense pride.

When Robbie arrived in Swarthmore at age five, his aunt Dorris brought him to Ray's door. Dorris's husband is related to Ray's grandfather. That day, she introduced the two and told Ray that Robbie would be staying with them from now on. Robbie wandered inside and the two sat there awkwardly until Robbie asked if he could play Ray's Nintendo. "I was like, oh, man. I don't know." Ray says he didn't want to share and then explodes into laughter.

But Robbie returned the next day and the next. Their bond grew from there. They would play basketball together for hours, and even after Ray went inside, he would still see Robbie practicing outside by himself. He also remembers Robbie's adaptability—he could fit in just as easily with his family in Chester as with the rich white folks that were their neighbors in Swarthmore. Robbie was constantly going from house to house, visiting everyone, from Swarthmore to nearby Media, where another black enclave is located, to Philadelphia and Wallingford. Ray recalls a time when his friend was having a hard time at college, and Robbie drove all the way to Cornell just to get him out of the house. Robbie was an eternal optimist, Ray tells me, an innocent.

Robbie always maintained a rosy exterior. "When you were in his presence," his friend Durrell says, "you could never really tell if anything was upsetting him. But deep down he had a lot going on."

One of his closest friends until he died, Durrell was in the eighth grade when his parents moved him from West Philadelphia to Wallingford. On his first or second day at Strath Haven Middle School, Robbie walked onto Durrell's school bus, introduced himself, and struck up a conversation. It was memorable because Robbie rode a different bus to his home in Swarthmore, several miles away from Durrell's new apartment in Wallingford. Durrell hadn't ridden a school bus before, only public transportation, and Robbie showed him how the bus system worked. Their connection was instant. They both loved playing sports, especially basketball. A few months later, they learned their families were already acquainted. Durrell's mom was originally from Chester, where she knew Robbie's family. They realized they'd probably seen each other as little kids and never realized it.

In high school, Durrell recalls, Robbie's mom was present, showing up to his basketball games and other events. Durrell didn't hear much about Robbie's father until college, when father and son began to rekindle their relationship. At the time, Robbie asked Durrell if he should continue speaking to his father. Durrell told him everybody deserved a second chance.

Robbie graduated from college and began to read voraciously, seemingly on a mission to understand where he came from. He started writing and shared it with friends. He began to reconsider his happy childhood in Swarthmore. He started to question the educational system and the school district that raised him, and the things we were taught as children. He wondered why he didn't learn about things like black history.

He also began to reevaluate his faith. Robbie's father was a pastor and he had been a lifelong Christian. Ray introduced Robbie to the works of Elijah Muhammad, and together they discussed figures like Martin Luther King Jr. and Malcolm X, whom Robbie idolized. They read the Bible together chapter by chapter and began to debate it.

"From my perspective, he almost started feeling guilty," Ray says, recalling Robbie's exploration of belief.

Around the time Robbie and I started exchanging messages, I noticed a change in the tone of his posts on Facebook. Always irreverent, they became politically conscious and were often about literature. Above a photo of the cover of Michelle Alexander's *The New Jim Crow*, he wrote, "Shout out to Ms. Michelle Alexander for creating a Masterful piece of informative literature . . . READ!!!! It isn't punishable by death anymore!" In school I was always outspokenly political, and he would sometimes speak to my mother about her life in South Africa. I imagined this burgeoning interest was one of the factors drawing us back together, after so many years, bridging the distance between us.

In 2012, compelled by a desire to give back, Durrell began teaching in Chester schools. Robbie was working at a window company and trying to get a massage therapy business off the ground. He was finding himself professionally, and he took a substitute teaching gig in a Chester middle school. Eventually that led to a job as assistant English teacher in the Chester Upland School District. He rented an apartment in Chester, even though he continued to spend time in Swarthmore. His uncle Butch offered to find him a better job, but Robbie demurred, insisting that his students needed him; they didn't have black male role models. He cared about them deeply and offered them life lessons in addition to classroom assignments. The students loved him in return. "He was super excited when those kids graduated from middle school," Durrell tells me.

In 2018, about two years after Robbie's murder, his mother took her life. Everyone I speak to attributes it partly to her grief over Robbie's death. I hear some stories about how it happened, and they haunt me. I imagine a grief without beginning or end. How difficult it is to not be swallowed by it.

I ask Durrell if he thinks Robbie would have ended up as a teacher.

"I think he would've went back to school and got his certification and done everything he needed to do," he says. "That was just Rob, he wanted to help in any way he could."

In many ways Swarthmore's inverse, Chester is Pennsylvania's oldest city. Originally inhabited by the Okehocking tribe, the city was the site of William Penn's landing in 1682. Penn incorporated Chester as a borough in 1701 as a refuge for Quakers. In

1866, Chester became a city. For much of its early history, it was an economic and social powerhouse due to its location along the Delaware River. It experienced its first boom after the Civil War, when its iron shipyards and textile industry attracted Irish, Polish, Italian, and African American migrant workers. These groups established long-standing communities that persisted through the twentieth century.

The First World War brought with it another major economic and population boom. New manufacturers, including Sun Shipbuilding, Sun Oil Company, Scott Paper Company, and Ford Motor Company nearly tripled the number of jobs available. European immigrants and African Americans taking part in the Great Migration nearly doubled Chester's population between 1910 and 1920. The massive growth predictably led to racial tension: black migrants faced discrimination and were pushed into substandard housing while local media stoked conflict by over-reporting "black on white" crimes. These tensions boiled over in 1917, when a group of four black friends, led by Arthur Thomas, encountered a white man named William McKinley while walking through a white neighborhood. An argument led to a fist-fight and McKinley was killed. In the subsequent days, whites attacked black people on the streets in retribution, and after four days of chaos, seven people had died.

The Second World War brought tens of thousands of new migrants to Chester's factories and its shipyards. During this time, Sun Shipbuilding became the largest private employer of African Americans in the country. The end of the war forced contractions in the local economy, and these same black workers were the first to lose their jobs. Prohibited from partaking in federal postwar housing and Veterans Affairs programs, Chester's black population was driven further into poverty, touching off a wave of white flight into the more prosperous surrounding suburbs, which during the 1950s led to the first population decrease in Chester's history. Black Chester residents were disallowed from migrating outward via discrimination in housing and job opportunities, and Chester became what it is today: an impoverished, majority-black city.

Until this time, Chester public schools had remained segregated due to the racial dynamics of the city. In the 1950s, the Chester School Board adopted an integration plan but allowed individual students to request transfers to schools outside their neighborhoods. The board routinely granted transfers to white students but not blacks, and by 1954, five of Chester's elementary schools were almost completely black. In response to the *Brown v. Board of Education* decision in 1954, and under pressure from the local branch of the NAACP, the board voted for complete integration in its schools, though de facto segregation, combined with surreptitious actions to maintain it, meant Chester schools remained solidly segregated.

By the 1960s, Chester had sunk even deeper into poverty as white flight continued and the city was drained of its middle class: 9.3 percent of its population was unemployed and the number of unemployed black people was even higher, at 14.2 percent. In total, Chester housed 60 percent of Delaware County residents on public assistance. Chester's schools reflected the city's poor conditions, with its mostly black elementary and junior high schools (of its sixteen schools only Chester High was integrated) in physical disrepair, with outdated textbooks and crumbling infrastructure.

Against the protests of residents and the NAACP, the Chester School Board maintained that it complied with *Brown v. Board of Education*, and so the battle to end de facto segregation in Chester began. By 1963 local protesters, led by organizer Stanley Branche, staged a series of direct actions in protest of segregation in Chester schools. In 1964, Malcolm X spoke in Chester on Branche's invitation. That year, Branche led a series of increasingly frequent demonstrations, boycotts, sit-ins, and marches that, by April, were occurring daily. The conflict reached its climax between April 22 and 26, when Pennsylvania state troopers joined forces with Chester police to arrest and brutalize dozens of protesters, forcing Governor William Scranton to intervene. Over the course of the 1963–64 protests, more than six hundred demonstrators were arrested. The severity of the events led civil rights leader James Farmer to dub Chester "the Birmingham of the North."

The demonstrations and subsequent media attention prompted action from the Pennsylvania Human Relations Commission, which issued an official order of desegregation to Chester schools. The board appealed the decision to the State Supreme Court, which upheld the desegregation order, but according to sociologist Christopher Mele, "Most of the recommendations remained unfulfilled through the 1970s, as the commission had limited authority to enforce them."

The decline of Chester's schools continues today. "The Chester-Upland school system's history is a history of U.S. segregation in miniature," wrote journalist Peter Greene in *Forbes* magazine in 2021. In 1994, Chester Upland School District was named the worst-performing school district in the state; in 2000 it was declared financially distressed, prompting its takeover by the Board of Control, which brought in a series of private companies to run its schools. In the following years, control of Chester schools was passed between outside entities and public receivers. It remains one of the lowest-performing districts in the state and has one of the highest dropout rates in the country. Today, Chester schools are being subsumed by charter schools, which, in 2015, received more state funding than Chester's public schools. This is the school system Robbie found when he began teaching years ago.

My mother worked as a kindergarten teacher for the School District of Philadelphia for the majority of my life. In her later years, she earned her principal certificate and began working as an administrator, first as a teaching coach and later as assistant director of the district's Head Start program. After meeting my father, she earned a full United Nations scholarship to the University of Pennsylvania's Graduate School of Education. While I was growing up, she sometimes expressed regret over not having chosen a more lucrative, prestigious career. The possibilities were nearly endless for her, but she felt called to service of underprivileged black children. She was intimately involved in the lives of her students, forming relationships with parents and family members, advocating for and protecting them, even when it fell outside the rules, like when she frequently broke up fistfights between students.

Her dedication to her job presented difficult choices for our family. As an employee, she was required to live within district lines, limiting us to the city. In Philadelphia, the number of well-performing schools was small, and my parents couldn't afford the neighborhoods where they were located. We would be able to test into one of the city's handful of magnet high schools, but there was no guarantee of admission. They found Yeadon, a nice community they could afford, and sent us to Lansdowne Friends School. For the entirety of her career, my mother used her best friend Lorna's address for school district correspondence. As I got older and started driving, she'd sometimes ask me to swing by Lorna's house in North Philadelphia to pick up her paychecks.

As I entered grade school and they could no longer afford private tuition, my mother did some research and came upon the Wallingford-Swarthmore School District. My parents thought long and hard about the price they'd pay in sending us to a mostly white school, examining the risk–benefit between cultural alienation and educational opportunity.

When I ask my father about this decision he pauses. "There aren't many good choices for black families," he says with resignation.

"So much of school segregation is structural—a result of decades of housing discrimination, of political calculations and the machinations of policy makers, of simple inertia. But I also [believe] that it is the choices of individual parents that uphold the system." Nikole Hannah-Jones wrote in her 2016 *New York Times* article about choosing a segregated school in New York City for her daughter. Hannah-Jones ultimately chose to resist this system and send her daughter to a segregated mostly black school, even though they had access to a better-performing, mostly white one.

The very same factors were at work for my parents in 1990s Philadelphia, and they chose the opposite. I press him a couple of times, but my father doesn't remember being conscious of their complicity in segregation. My mother isn't around to ask, but I have a hard time believing that the thought never entered her mind. I wonder how she squared this decision, or if she did it at all.

Before my early thirties, I'd never thought seriously about the possibility of having children, much less where I would send them to school. On the verge of motherhood at thirty-seven years old, exposed to years of research and findings about the impact of segregation, I don't think I will make the same choices as my parents. But would I have made the same choice they did nearly forty years ago? I don't know. Do I judge them for it? Yes.

Due to the long legacy of segregation in the United States, black families face similar issues across the country. However, due to its particular set of laws and administration, the situation in Pennsylvania is particularly acute. Pennsylvania has five hundred school districts. Delaware County alone, home to just over five hundred thousand people, houses fifteen. The high number of districts in Pennsylvania has allowed segregation to proliferate.

The landmark 1974 Supreme Court decision in the case of *Milliken v. Bradley* overturned a lower court order to desegregate Detroit public schools by also redrawing its surrounding suburban school districts. In essence, the 5–4 decision provided a massive loophole to *Brown v. Board of Education* by asserting that desegregation could not be enforced across district lines. "This decision significantly diminished the capacity of courts and governments to integrate schools and cleared the way for district borders to be used as lawful tools of segregation," wrote the organization EdBuild in their 2016 study of the fifty most-segregated district borders in the United States. Of the fifty borders identified in the study, six were located in Pennsylvania.

In 2015, US Secretary of Education Arne Duncan announced that Pennsylvania had the widest spending gap between rich and poor school districts, a situation that he asserted must be remedied. Ranked forty-fifth in the nation for state education funding in 2021, Pennsylvania forces individual districts to contribute heavily to school funding with local property taxes. In 2014, low-income Pennsylvania districts spent more than $4,000 less on students per pupil, and in total $4.4 billion was needed to bring all students up to academic standards.

Such factors led six Pennsylvania school districts, the Pennsylvania Association of Rural and Small Schools, the NAACP Pennsylvania State Conference, and a group of public school parents to sue the state of Pennsylvania in 2014 for failure to provide a "thorough and efficient" public school system. One of the six plaintiff school districts was William Penn, where I used to live. In 2023, Commonwealth Court Judge Renee Cohn Jubilerer ruled the situation of unequal funding unconstitutional. How Pennsylvania will choose to remedy the situation remains unclear, but the decision is widely seen as a first step. Dan Urevick-Ackelsberg, the Public Interest Law Center attorney who represented the plaintiffs, said, "This is an earthquake that will reverberate for the children of Pennsylvania." In the meantime, students will continue to suffer and some, like my parents and others, will seek their own solutions.

A 2022 index by the Century Foundation found that the Philadelphia–Delaware County area is the most segregated in the country for Latino children and ranks ninth nationwide for black–white segregation. In 2025, spending per weighted student in the 3,589-student Wallingford-Swarthmore School District was $16,756, compared to $10,229 each for the 6,730 students in Chester Upland. Chester Upland had a total of $13,523,422 in cyber charter expenditure compared to $566,132 in Wallingford-Swarthmore.

With such unequal educational opportunities often existing within miles of one another, it's no wonder parents would go to costly and often risky lengths to establish residency in our region's affluent school districts. Little discussed while I was in school, in later years I came to learn that a large percentage of my black classmates came from neighboring districts, like Chester and Philadelphia. Their families faced incredibly steep costs to send their children to Wallingford-Swarthmore.

Vaughn and I were in high school together for a couple of years, where he was a star of the track and soccer teams. He also grew up in the Historically Black Neighborhood, where he and Robbie were close. He also lived on a street populated by his family, and across the street from his grandfather.

"While I did grow up surrounded by people that looked like me, when I stepped outside of that zone, I definitely felt perceptions and some judgments," he tells me.

He recalls visiting Strath Haven High School after he'd graduated and was enrolled in a college-prep program at Phillips Exeter Academy in New Hampshire. At the high school, he ran into his former math teacher, who seemed shocked to hear what he was doing. "She basically insinuated that she thought I would be working at McDonald's," he says, "which was puzzling because I did well in her class."

He laments the way black athletes weren't supported by school officials, who expected him to be a superstar and never make mistakes. He was reminded constantly that he was replaceable. Our athletics program was a great pride in our community, with Strath Haven's football team winning two back-to-back state championships while I was a student. Yet, of all the black athletes Vaughn knew, including Robbie, few ended up at top universities, unlike their white peers. Instead, many of those black student athletes he knew ended up incarcerated or worse. "The school system was all too happy to say, 'Hey, play sports!' What you do after that, we don't know."

The first time we spoke, Vaughn was living in a home he purchased in the Historically Black Neighborhood with his wife and two daughters, who attended a school in the Wallingford-Swarthmore School District. In first grade, one of his daughters displayed a stutter while learning to read. A teaching assistant strongly recommended that she be put on a special education track to address her speech issues. Vaughn and his wife recognized that once their daughter was put on the special education track, it would be difficult to reverse. Instead, they chose to address the issue on their own. It worked.

They soon realized that their daughters were gifted academically. Both received praise from their elementary-school teachers and scored extremely well on IQ tests. When they heard, secondhand, about the school's gifted and talented program, they were surprised to hear that it existed. Vaughn's wife contacted the administrators herself.

"We basically had to force our way in," he says. "How striking: Here you have two children who sound like geniuses, and the only recommendation they got was for something punitive.

"When I think about the school district and I think about Robbie, it's like, how is someone like that not here anymore? What could have been done to change their trajectory? With someone as talented and as gifted as Rob was in many areas of life, there could have been different opportunities for him."

A few months after I spoke with him, I heard from his neighbors that Vaughn and his family had relocated out of state.

In fifth grade, I had been at Swarthmore-Rutledge School for a year and a half and felt, if an outsider, mostly happy. My intelligence had always been recognized by my teachers, but at Swarthmore, I was allowed to flourish. I received an appointment and was taken to a room on the first floor of my school to answer logic problems and identify colorful shapes on flash cards. I felt special; I found the experience fun. I emerged with an IEP and was put on the gifted and talented track. My teachers gave me extra assignments and spent time with me outside of class.

I couldn't learn enough. I relished homework assignments, anticipating the praise I would receive after completing them to perfection. At some point around this time, I received the nickname "Dictionary." My favorite teacher was Mrs. Jones, who took a special interest in me, challenged me, and claimed me as her own. Outside of my family, I'd never known a protector like her.

But it was in the comfort of her class that I experienced my first racial trauma. It was show-and-tell day, and a boy with whom I'd begun a friendship brought in a collection of trophies and ribbons. In between lessons, I approached the display on the side of the class. All of a sudden, my friend appeared between me and the shelf. "Back off, black girl," he snarled at me.

I was stunned, confused. Mrs. Jones ran to my side and comforted me. She corrected the boy and told the class why it was wrong to say such things. By the end of the discussion, the boy was in tears. I guess some reparation was made, but I felt foolish—for believing that we were friends and for thinking I could behave like I was any other kid in that class.

From that point on, I started to close myself off. I adopted a stony, impenetrable expression that has stuck with me to this day. I didn't offer of myself unless I was invited. My sense of self fragmented—between the person I knew myself to be—the person I was to my family and to other black people—and the person who was received by that place.

These mixed messages spawned my experience of "twoness." My self-worth shifted completely depending on my company, and my sense of self was completely absent. I became defensive. I developed the belief—which still exists in me—that any acceptance I experience is temporary, and it's only a matter of time before I am humiliated, rejected, or worse. This year was my twentieth high school reunion and I still find myself unlearning the harmful lessons that that place taught me about myself.

My parents focused relentlessly on our education to the exclusion of nearly all other considerations. Friends, boyfriends, activities were only discussed for how much they aided or interfered with our schooling. The psychological traumas of living in Swarthmore felt like the price of achieving the future I wanted.

I was focused on getting out, which entailed acceptance to a good college and then a good job, securing myself the future I wanted. We were made constantly aware that, as black children, we would be subject to harsher punishments than our peers. I avoided drugs and alcohol and all situations that involved legal exposure. I drove carefully; I never went to big parties, and when there was alcohol around, I was always the least intoxicated, keeping my wits about me in case the situation went south. I went home early. I didn't speak out of turn or draw attention to myself.

Over time, I made friends with the children in my activities, in my art classes and AP seminars—bookish, nerdy, and alternative kids. Though I was accepted and loved by them, I found myself on the periphery, left out of many social events or too uncomfortable to fully participate. Many of my most salient memories of high school are of me alone in my room listening to music, writing, and reading. I spent many Friday nights at the local Border's Books and Music, where I made my way through the literature shelves and kept up with all the periodicals. This is where I found my solitude, where I discovered that the tools of self-confidence were accessible to me if only I found silence enough to listen. That is how I became a writer. Nearly everything I have now that I hold dear, Swarthmore gave to me. I still do not know how to reconcile what it took.

The last time I saw Robbie in high school I was sitting outside the building waiting for the bus. It was after a sports game and there were only a few other kids around. I was reading a book and waiting for my ride when I saw him from the corner of my eye, striding confidently toward the front door. I felt the urge to say hello, but my shyness gripped me at the last moment. I felt suddenly afraid, because he was so much more popular, that he wouldn't return my greeting, a serious humiliation in high school. The several rungs that separated us on the social ladder grew miles apart in that instant. Robbie glanced toward me and, perhaps taking my cue, looked back up and straight ahead of him.

The last time we saw each other was in the shopping mall near my family home, where years ago we'd spent Fridays playing at grown-ups, haunting the food court, and spending our first dollars. I can't pinpoint the exact year, but it was sometime between 2007, when I graduated from college, and 2012, when my mother died. She and I were walking arm in arm. I'd returned home for a short trip. Robbie and I were in our early twenties. We had been out of high school for a few years; we hadn't seen each other in as long. My mother probably called to him; I would not have had the courage. She embraced him excitedly, gushed over how big he'd gotten, how handsome he'd become. She steered me through the interaction that day, bridging the gulf between us. I was relieved by her intervention, and he seemed so, too. He seemed happy. It was shortly after that meeting that we started trading messages. The gap between us had begun to close, and then just like that, he was gone.

In the years after his death, I dream of Robbie occasionally. The dreams become more vivid when I begin to write about him.

In one dream, he pops up in the form of several creatures and I understand it as him trying to communicate with me as a snake, a rabbit, a friendly dog. I'm comforted by these animals, and by the knowledge that he cares enough to send me signs.

I dream that I visit Robbie in an old but tidy mobile home. He shows me around the living room proudly, pointing to an inviting easy chair that sits just in front of a large window. The whole place is awash in beautiful golden light, and I feel a permeating sense of peace. The place is modest, but it seems comfortable and safe. Everything is all right, he seems to be telling me.

I dream that I am at a summer camp with Robbie. It's a beautiful place with nice facilities, and at the end there is a catered party with music and dancing. Then my parents show up, and we find out that Robbie isn't who we thought he was. He has done all kinds of horrible things, including that he has run over a baby with his car. It's shocking, and all the warm feelings I felt toward him before are deflated immediately. I'm distraught. Everyone is disappointed. It's horrible, and after a while, we make an effort to forget him. We eventually do. When I wake up, I'm left with what feels like loss two times over, and I remember how forgetting is in some ways the worst punishment we can inflict as humans.

In 2017, on tour for my debut novel, I returned to Swarthmore for a reading at the college. As is often true of first novels, mine drew heavily from my own life and included a fictionalized version of my hometown as the main character's own.

It was in that novel that I finally confided my feelings about having grown up there, about the racism and alienation I experienced as a child, the severe loneliness the place bred in me. Friends and family expressed surprise at those feelings; I always seemed so well-adjusted, they told me.

I'd imagined the reading as my chance to finally voice how that place had truly made me feel. I'd planned to confront my former community with the harsh truth of their seemingly perfect hometown. I was the outcast who'd returned to her home a success. This would be my moment of triumph.

The reading was held in the brand-new campus hotel. As I

crossed the unfamiliar parking lot to a building I'd never seen before, my resolve began to erode. A sign directed me to the hotel's conference room, where several rows of seats had been arranged in front of a podium, each one of them filled with the white, silver-haired parents of my former classmates and friends. I'd been to their houses, seen them at soccer games, learned their secrets, seen them angry and sad. As I walked to the podium, they smiled at me and shook my hand proudly. In the front row sat the mother of one of the most popular girls in my grade, a blond soccer player who treated me with silent disdain. As I spoke, her mother beamed at me with fondness. I felt my nerves calm, along with my anger toward them.

I read the few pages I'd planned, then took questions from the audience. A couple of weeks ago, as I drove solo across Pennsylvania for a reading in Pittsburgh, white supremacists had marched in Charlottesville and clashed with counterprotesters in the streets, claiming the life of Heather Heyer. Across the country, Confederate statues and street signs were beginning to be torn down. I told the crowd that we'd fixated on statues because we were unable to confront the much deeper problems in our society. "In some ways, I'm a statue for this town," I declared to knowing murmurs. The Q&A rolled on.

At the end of the program, a woman at the back of the room raised her hand. She looked about forty, South Asian with mahogany skin; she identified herself as a professor. She asked if I could reflect on the racism I experienced in Swarthmore growing up. She and her husband had moved there for their jobs, and she told me matter-of-factly that they had to pull their children out of Wallingford-Swarthmore School District because of the racism they faced from their classmates.

I jumbled out an answer, parts of my prepared thoughts and some observations from the moment. At the end, everyone cheered. The woman looked satisfied. It was far from the moment of triumph I'd envisioned, but I felt something much larger that had eluded me for so many years—acceptance—and, along with it, shame.

When the reading closed, we moved across the hallway to the bookstore, where I signed my name and wrote cheery messages to my former classmates and their parents on the title page of my book. Later that evening, I walked next door to the hotel's restaurant with my father, two of my friends' mothers, and Mrs. Jones, who still bristled with the energy of an elementary-school teacher. She didn't appear to have aged a day. We ordered wine and fancy appetizers and joked and laughed about all the years that had passed since I last saw them. About how much had changed and how little.

Toward the end of the night, Mrs. Jones leaned into me. I'd planned to thank her for all she did for me growing up, but instead she beat me to it. Mrs. Jones adopted two daughters who were dark-skinned and of Latino heritage and stood out like a sore thumb in our town. She thanked me for always being kind to her daughter, who I'd heard had been bullied in school. I saw her only occasionally, when Mrs. Jones would bring her into class for short visits. I don't remember going out of my way to be kind to her, just treating her like anyone else. But I guess that was Mrs. Jones's point. I didn't tell her how her daughter's brown skin, her familiar discomfort with her surroundings, made me feel less alone. I smiled at her. "Of course," I said.

Not long after this visit, I start hearing a rumor about our high school. One of my friends has a much younger half sister who is a student at Strath Haven High. On one of my visits, she mentions that the sister takes classes in trailers located on the school property.

In 1999, when we began high school, the school had undergone major construction and we were the first class to begin school in the completely new building. She mentions, in the offhand manner in which revelations often present themselves, that she had heard that the building had been built intentionally small so that the district would not have to enroll students from Chester.

I mention the rumor at dinner at the home of another high school friend. Without a bit of hesitation, her mother tells me that she was present at student-teacher meetings years ago where parents discussed it.

My friend Katie tells me that she decided on her career path during our last year at Strath Haven, when we volunteered at Chester High School as part of our senior service project. During that week, we cleaned trash from the schoolyard and painted a mural in one of the hallways. I remembered feeling awkward about the arrangement but at home in the environment. The school reminded me of the ones my mother had taught at all my life and of the public school in Yeadon I'd briefly attended before moving to Swarthmore. I was glad to see other black faces and exchanged furtive smiles with them in the hallways. The experience was a revelation for Katie, who realized how differently we lived, even though the school was only a few minutes' walk from her home. She's worked as a public-school teacher in Philadelphia's inner city ever since graduating from college. Sometime around then, she asked me what it was like growing up in Swarthmore as a black person. Even though we'd always been close, I felt from then on that she saw me in a different way—saw the whole me in a way none of my white classmates ever did. Partly for this reason, she remains one of my best friends.

Though they all occupied different social strata, all of my friends remember Robbie fondly. My brother and father make it to the funeral and tell me about the throngs of people spilling out of the church, all the people who loved Robbie and were stunned by the injustice of his murder. My high school class establishes a GoFundMe that raises more than $14,000 for his son, and other classmates establish a scholarship fund for student athletes at our high school. Even in death, his reputation as everyone's friend holds true.

I speak to Liza, another high school friend. At the time she is living in her childhood home, having moved back a few years ago. In high school, she was my rebellious friend, prone to punk aesthetics and radical politics.

"Any time I'm in Swarthmore for any reason," she tells me, "I know that people are going to look down on me because I'm not a doctor or a lawyer." She worked as a vendor at the local farmers market for a time, where she'd run into people we grew up with who treated her dismissively. "It's been a lot of that," she says.

She's delighted that I'm writing this essay. She tells me that Swarthmore is undergoing something of a reckoning. The younger residents—including some of our former classmates—are more willing to openly discuss Swarthmore's racist past. However, she tells me, there is little recognition of how that racism is still alive and active today.

A few minutes into our conversation, I mention the rumor. "I heard that the school was built smaller than it was originally intended—"

"Yeah," she cuts me off before I can finish my sentence, "to keep Chester kids out."

I speak with Mr. Ellis, a former teacher at Strath Haven High School. I don't know which is a mobile or a landline, so I call with the intention of setting up an appointment for a formal interview. I have a process for conducting these, which normally entails a lengthy introduction and disclaimer, and I record all my interviews for my records. Once he picks up and we exchange greetings (he says he's followed my career in the press), he starts talking, alighting on one topic to the next, and I barely have time to take notes.

He tells me that he didn't know Robbie personally, but he taught in Chester for many years and knew members of his family. When I recount the manner in which Robbie died, he tells me that he's heard many similar stories of people murdered, their cases unsolved and seemingly random. It was common. He tells me about students who didn't show up to class one day. He'd ask their classmates what happened, and they'd respond casually, "He got shot," with a smile on their face. The kids see so much, he tells me, way beyond what the average suburban kid can imagine.

He tells me about a female student of his who was struggling, whom he offered to help after school. In response, the girl looked at him in absolute horror. Later, he found out that she had had a sexual relationship with another teacher in middle school. That everyone—students, teachers, administrators included—knew about it, and no one did anything. The teacher was never fired. One day at a party, Mr. Ellis brought it up loud enough for them all to hear. They simply looked on and smiled, saying nothing. He pauses at this moment to spell the teacher's name for me.

Then the energy shifts on the other line. His voice slows and becomes deeper. He tells me there's something else that he can't prove, but "I know it in my bones to be true." He repeats the rumor to me, almost verbatim.

He tells me that, at the time the new building was being built, there had been talk of shutting down the Chester Upland School District. Pennsylvania law states that if that happens, the students must be enrolled in nearby districts, but if the building was full, they couldn't accept more students. So the decision had been made to build the school small. I ask him if he can prove it.

"No school board member would put this down in writing, they're too smart for that," he says. "The public is lied to all the time by school board members. But when you live in the milieu, there are things you just know."

Aside from these incidents, I hear the rumor repeated a handful of other times. I repeat it to my brother, who looks at me plaintively. "Everybody knows that," he says.

I have found no written record to confirm that this decision was made. What I have found are pieces that, when assembled, form a picture. The rumors—which include several independent verifications—are pieces. During the nineties, when the new Strath Haven High School building was being planned and constructed, Chester Upland School District was on the brink of closure.

Another piece: Article XIII, 24 PS § 13-1311 of Pennsylvania Statutes holds that, upon the closure of a school due to low attendance, poor conditions, or any other reason, "the pupils who belong to the same shall be assigned to other schools, or upon cause shown, be permitted to attend schools in other districts."

In the picture, I float through, a chosen one. From this perspective, my traumas seem insignificant. The safety of my position, juxtaposed with the suffering of so many, is hard to rectify. And Robbie straddles the canvas—prized and discarded, safe and endangered all at once. In two dimensions, such movement is difficult to render. He is a blur, a phantom. A ghost.

In January 2023, shortly after the new year, I return to Swarthmore chasing Robbie. I book a room at the Swarthmore Inn and stay right above the bookstore where I read in 2017. It's the first time I've been here in years, and my longest stay since I left at eighteen. The window of my hotel room—comfortable yet modest enough for a Quaker—overlooks the train station and the town village, where my only high school boyfriend—a black skater I met in art class—lived. At night, the train's foghorn blares outside my window, triggering a deep memory of its ominous sound somewhere within me.

I have been married to my husband, André, for eight years. A few years ago, I shared with him that I wanted a child, and after a few months of trying, I am finally pregnant and blissful, but not yet showing. I started feeling him early, around fourteen weeks, a tiny fluttering deep in my abdomen that bloomed into a tumbling sensation, like driving too fast over a hill. I learn that my body's immune system carefully calibrates so as not to reject the fetus like a virus or a parasite. It's a startling realization, the fact that a totally separate life-form is growing inside you, but from the moment it started happening, it's filled me with a sense of reassurance and calm deeper than any I've known.

On the plane ride over, I fainted shortly after takeoff on my way to the bathroom, still unaccustomed to the demands a growing baby placed on my body. As I came to, I informed the worried flight attendants that I was five months pregnant, and their tone immediately shifted to satisfied recognition. After they fed me coffee cake and orange juice and checked my vitals, I told them I was expecting a boy (a detail that seems incidental, at most, to me), and they told me that's why I passed out. Boys always give you more trouble, they said, smiling. I was wheeled out of the airport by a young black woman who grew up in Philly and later moved to "The County" for school. She loved living there, she told me. Compared to Philly, it was great. She told me she spent New Year's Eve in church. "God bless you," she said, and hugged me as we parted ways outside.

I'm told to watch for fetal activity in the following days. If there was a decrease, or if I experienced a number of symptoms, I'm to go to the nearest emergency room. I felt him a few hours after I landed, while I was resting, and I was reminded of the resilience of human life.

I drive to a tidy apartment block a couple of towns over to meet Timothy, who was two years below me in school. He greets me at the door along with his wife, who's on maternity leave after just having given birth to their youngest daughter. Their oldest is an adorable toddler with his mother's smile and Timothy's spunk. She greets me warmly, shows me her toys, and chatters excitedly from the living room while her father and I sit at the dining room table and talk.

Timothy told me his story a few years ago after a night out with friends. We'd gone out drinking, and at the end of the night he relayed the details of his time in Swarthmore over cheesesteaks at two in the morning. It had stuck with me since then, and soon after I started writing this essay, I knew I had to speak to him again.

Timothy grew up in Chester with two younger brothers and

his mother, who worked in administration at Chester High School. They lived on the safer, more middle-class east side of Chester, where Timothy exhibited promise and was placed in the gifted and talented program. He loved the community there, which included his extended family, and he was proud of Chester's history and its involvement in the Civil Rights Movement. When we speak, he mentions the years Martin Luther King Jr. spent in the city as a student at Crozer Theological Seminary. Timothy was enrolled in a private school until the third grade, when his mother began homeschooling him for a year and a half. He then enrolled in a public school in Chester, where he had a hard time because he wasn't from the same neighborhood as his classmates. They looked for other options.

In the seventh grade, his mother decided they would undertake the burdensome task of sending him and his brothers to schools in the Wallingford-Swarthmore School District. To establish residency, they'd need to rent an apartment within the district lines, and they found one minutes from our middle school in Wallingford. According to Timothy, their time there was "hell." In addition to her Chester High job, his mother also worked a part-time job in retail to afford the rent. As the only black family in their apartment complex, their landlord targeted them with accusations and threats, increasing the stress on their household.

Soon after they moved in, Timothy remembers receiving letters from the Wallingford-Swarthmore School District. The letters notified them that they needed to reside full-time within the district lines and they couldn't spend time in Chester. Their Chester address wasn't listed on any official documents and they did not report it to the school officials. They surmised that a school district representative had been following Timothy and his brother home from school back to the Chester house. Though disturbed, the family complied so as not to cause more trouble. This would be just the beginning of the harsh treatment they'd receive from school officials.

At Strath Haven Middle School, Timothy was required to begin foreign language instruction, which other students started in the sixth grade. As a new seventh grader, he was at a marked disadvantage and began struggling in class. Rather than offering support, his teacher antagonized him, calling him out to his classmates and accusing him of cutting corners. About three months into his time there, Timothy had had enough. When she began to berate him in class, he responded with anger. He wished he'd blown up the school, he muttered.

Immediately, Timothy was shuffled to the principal's office. The police were called. His mother was at work, and he told the officers that he had to pick his younger brother up from school. Instead of arranging a pickup with his mother, the officers escorted him to the elementary school and brought them both back to the middle school. It was only then that they called to inform his mother. Held in the principal's office for hours, Timothy wept uncontrollably, knowing he was in trouble but unaware of just how deeply.

This all occurred on a Friday afternoon. By that evening, he was sent to juvenile detention. At twelve, Timothy was the youngest one there. He was small for his age—around four feet tall—with a giant Afro. As he was escorted into the juvenile detention center, he remembers encountering a group of girls outside who laughed at him. "You don't belong here," they told him, and though embarrassed, he felt relieved to hear someone else validate what he knew to be true.

Inside, he recognized some familiar faces from Chester, including some friends' parents who worked as guards. They looked after him. Everyone else left him alone. For the first two days, he slept alone in a cell. He remembers smelling of salt because of how much he cried. At first, he refused to take showers, afraid of what he'd been told happened there in prison. Eventually, another boy told him he would be safe. He was moved outside his cell and slept in the common area on a mat on the floor. He felt better there. For a while, he held out hope that he would be found innocent, but by Monday, after seeing other children emerge from their court appointments screaming and cursing in disappointment, he started to worry.

In court it emerged that in her statement to the police, Timothy's teacher alleged that during class he'd made a disturbance, standing on desks and assaulting his classmates. On the witness stand, the teacher was forced to admit she had fabricated those details. Timothy was lucky to have a family friend who was a lawyer, who defended him in his trial. If he hadn't, he says, things would have ended up very differently. On Tuesday, he was released. "I couldn't get out of there fast enough," he says.

Timothy was removed from the teacher's class, but she remained employed at the school, as did the administrators who presided over his incarceration. To make matters worse, he later learned that, the year before this happened, a white kid had brought a hit list and a gun to school. That student received a suspension. When Timothy's family found out, they discussed suing, but in the end, they decided it was best to put the whole episode behind them. Timothy wonders what would have happened if they'd pursued justice. "I guess I would have sued the school and left," he speculates, "and who knows who I'd be?"

Around 2019, Timothy listened to a podcast on the Central Park Five case while he was driving. As the narrator detailed the experience of the young boys, railroaded by the police, forced into false confessions, and eventually jailed on Rikers Island, Timothy started to experience a panic attack. He pulled his car over. As he recovered, he realized how deeply that incident continued to affect him. He was forced to confront the injustice of what had happened to him and how similar it was to the now-exonerated Central Park men. "I wasn't in jail for twenty years, but it's the same thing. White [person] lied. I go to jail. Nothing happens to her, and I'm left to deal with everything."

At home, the harassment from their landlord became so unbearable that they moved to another apartment in Swarthmore. Rents were considerably higher there, so Timothy's mother took on a different part-time job with even longer hours. Every day, she left home at seven in the morning and returned at eleven at night, leaving Timothy in charge of his two younger brothers.

Despite his increased responsibilities, Timothy's grades slowly improved. The black students and teachers rallied around him in response to the incident and he finally started to make friends. But the racism he faced in Swarthmore intensified as he grew older. He and his brothers were stopped by police officers for offenses like throwing water balloons and walking near a post office. He recounts an incident when a Swarthmore College student made racist threats toward his younger brother in the town's pizza shop. Though white customers filled the tiny shop's handful of booths, none of them said anything.

As we speak, Timothy's daughter occasionally wanders into the room grinning and baby-talking, apparently eager to join our conversation. After meeting in college, Timothy and his wife settled here, in a town not far from Swarthmore but more economically and racially mixed. His wife cradles their newborn in the living room. "I'd probably feel more safe if I put her in day care in Chester than Swarthmore," he tells me, "but I also want to give them the best opportunity possible."

Robbie's uncle, Butch, has been suffering with a sinus infection for the past couple of weeks. His wife, Dorris, has been in and out of the hospital for the last few months. When I arrive, Dorris has just been discharged from a rehab center. She's too weak to come down and speak to me. As we sit in their kitchen, I can hear the click and whir of Dorris's asthma machine from upstairs.

Butch greets me at the front door just after nine thirty in the morning. He walks me inside, past a table that faces their front door displaying photos of Robbie. One is a large portrait of him sporting his huge, charismatic grin. When I first entered their home after his death in 2019, I had to fight back tears at the sight of it. Today, it is slightly yellowed, faded over the years, and I pass by it without the same pang of grief.

Butch doesn't flinch when I bring out my voice recorder and ask if I can record our conversation; he must be used to it by now with the spate of coverage in the local papers. It takes very little to get him talking, and as soon as we begin, he describes Robbie's departure from the July Fourth block party and the manner in which the news of his death slowly wended its way to them—first to Robbie's friends, then to police officers, then to Dorris's brother, who told him. No one could believe it. Butch then notified Robbie's father, who was at another party with relatives. "All you could hear was hollering," he says, "it was so numbing, it was like I was walking on air."

He tells me about the outpouring of sympathy they received in the aftermath of Robbie's death. A young woman in the neighborhood who went to high school with us wrote to Butch about how she was teased because she used a wheelchair. Every day, she said, Robbie would give her a hug. "He was a loving person, a gentleman," he says.

Butch's daughter Danielle emerges from upstairs. I brought a quiche with me from the produce market down Providence Road, and with little conversation, she warms it in the oven, arranges place settings before us, and offers us orange juice. From my first visit, when I showed up at their door as little more than a stranger, they've taken me in with unfailing warmth and generosity. Back then, Dorris arranged a meal for me with leftovers from a family dinner: meat, mac and cheese, greens, and soda. Each time I've arrived since then, unannounced, they've done the same. Their kindness is axiomatic, and it's easy to see how they would take Robbie in without a second thought and raise him as their own.

Robbie's mother was an educator, a gifted one, Butch says, who also struggled with drugs. She was using a lot when Robbie was a toddler, when Butch and Dorris got a call that he was found wandering around in a parking lot late at night, playing. One night, Dorris's sister's husband went and picked him up. The next time they got a call, Butch picked him up. He asked Dorris, Why don't we just keep him? It was obvious that Robbie's mom couldn't take care of him, and they reasoned that it would be better that he stayed with them until she could get herself together. They agreed in writing that when she was fit and able, she was free to take him back.

When Robbie was around ten years old, he went down to Virginia over vacation to visit her. During the visit, his mother decided she would keep him. Butch and Dorris were disappointed, but they honored the agreement they'd set forward. Robbie started calling, asking to come back. His father, who had been in and out of his life, found out that he was in his mother's care and took her to court. Butch and Dorris argued in court on Robbie's mother's behalf that she should retain custody. However, Robbie's mother and father argued so viciously during the proceedings that the judge took the decision out of their hands. Robbie was summoned to the courtroom and asked where he wanted to live. He told the judge he loved both his parents, but that he wanted to live with Butch and Dorris, and he was remanded to their care.

From then on, Butch's daughters accepted Robbie as a brother.

They loved him unconditionally. But they sometimes questioned the preferential treatment he received from their parents. They didn't realize how much Robbie had to overcome at a young age. Butch reveals that one of Robbie's mother's boyfriends molested him. He recalls trying to open the door to the bathroom and Robbie wouldn't let him come inside. Later, he realized why.

In Butch and Dorris's care, he was able to overcome the various obstacles of his childhood. "He loved living in Swarthmore," Butch says. When Robbie decided to move back to Chester, Dorris asked why he'd want to go back there. "I said to Dorr, he needs to get out on his own. He needs to grow."

They tell me that he loved practicing dancing to Michael Jackson songs in the basement. He never let anyone watch, and after hours had passed, he would come upstairs sweating, a smile on his face. They tell me that Robbie loved old people. "He had great respect for his elders," Butch says. This is something that nearly everyone who knew Robbie tells me. He loved spending hours around older people, learning from them, caring for them, and making them smile. They tell me about basketball games and vacations. Dinners with friends. Funny stories. He was everybody's friend. They light up when they remember him. And then the light dims.

I ask Butch what the neighborhood was like back in the day. One of the first families in the Historically Black Neighborhood, their property was bought by Butch's grandparents and has been in his family ever since, though the house itself is new. Butch informs me with some measure of pride that theirs was the first house in Swarthmore to be torn down completely and built again on the same lot. Butch's brother remembers when the streets were still dirt roads. Back then, they grew grapes, apples, and nectarines in their yard. The neighborhood was still black then, and they never locked their doors unless they went on vacation. Sometimes they slept downstairs with the door open. Back then, Butch tells me, if you disrespected a neighbor, you got two beatings: one from the neighbor and one from your parents for disrespecting the neighbor. "And I probably got more beatings than anyone in the neighborhood," he says with a laugh.

For a moment, I'm able to envision how my life might have unfolded differently if I'd grown up here, just three blocks from where I was raised, but a world away. How many of my early heartbreaks, hang-ups, and insecurities would have been eliminated, or at least blunted, by the love of this community?

I ask if they remember where the house was that Robbie lived in with his mother so many years ago. They can't remember an exact address, but they tell me it's somewhere near the soccer stadium, toward the southern border of Chester just north of the waterfront. I could stay and chat with them for much longer, but I have to be off. After the first day, the pace of the visit has been demanding, but the activity has been good for the baby. I feel him dancing as Danielle starts clearing the plates. I thank them for their kindness and walk out the front door, Robbie's portrait smiling at me as I bid them farewell.

I know I have to go to the place where Robbie died, even though every cell in my body begs me not to. Robbie's friends tell me they feel the same way, like Timothy, who stopped visiting his barber because it was near the intersection where Robbie was shot. "It could have been me in that box," he told me. Since I landed, I've thought of every possible excuse for not going and knocked them all down, one by one, over the past week. When the time comes, my body guides me there as if by rote.

I program my GPS for Subaru Park. It takes me down Providence Road and past the turnoff for our old house on Strath Haven Avenue. Then I pass Katie's neighborhood, and before I know it, the street signs change to blue.

Soon, the once-great Victorian homes that housed Chester's manufacturing barons give way to decaying row houses, empty lots, and the occasional corner store. Every few blocks, I see a memorial mural on the broadside of a building, a printed banner hanging between the banisters of a front porch with the photo of a loved one, two dates bookending their too-short life. Poverty has a different phenotype depending on its geography. In New York, it's people crowded vertically into tall apartment blocks and aging tenements. In South Africa, the poor live in improvised housing made from scrap metal. In California, it's tents huddled together under an overpass; a car or RV, its windows covered in yellowing paper or crowded with piles of belongings. In the neighborhood near the stadium where Robbie grew up, poverty is empty space and blight—a negative reminding us what was once there.

I drive down Second Street and can see the Delaware River just a few blocks away. I stop at Calvary Baptist Church and snap a picture of the building, and a historical marker that informs visitors that Martin Luther King Jr. used to minister there.

I take a left on the road to the Covanta incineration plant and see its smokestacks, dormant today, towering over the handful of row houses. There's barely anything here. I cross train tracks littered with garbage and encounter a group of children of varying shades of brown playing on either side of my vehicle. They are laughing and jostling over two simple toy airplanes made of wood. Up the block, a couple fixes a car. I imagine Robbie roaming around these disused blocks, looking for someone to play with.

I drive to the end of the block, turn around, and head back north. It's just a few more short blocks to Third and Kerlin Streets. The street is empty except for a couple of scattered pedestrians. I feel out of place, worried I'll attract attention. I slow the car to a crawl, slow enough to snap a picture of the used-car lot and abandoned warehouse on my phone. I picture unseen eyes watching the car slow, watching me raise my phone behind the windshield. My behavior could be unusual or threatening. I think of the life inside me. What could be gained, I think, by parking my car and communing with these empty buildings? I don't know if I'm doing the right thing, but I press the gas pedal. I keep driving.

I speak with Jeannine Osayande at her home in the Historically Black Neighborhood of Swarthmore (HBNS). The three-story wood-frame house has been in her family for five generations;

it's the home she was brought to as a baby and lived in all her life. She leads me through her living room, colorfully festooned with photos, warm printed fabrics, and Christmas decorations, to her kitchen, which looks out onto the central block of homes bounded by Bowdoin, Kenyon, and Union Avenues. It's a damp, gray January day, unseasonably warm.

Jeannine is a West African dance instructor, storyteller, and oral historian. With silver-flecked locs and smooth skin, she looks to have barely aged in the roughly fifteen years since I last saw her. Her children were a couple of years ahead of me in school, I remember them as smart and levelheaded. Jeannine tells me that they were teased as hippies for their vegetarian diets and for sporting the same locs as their mother. She has the presentation of a performer; she speaks assertively, her vowels slightly rounded with the distinctive Delaware County accent that turns *a*s to short *eh*s, all punctuated with occasional outbursts of boisterous laughter and dance-like movements.

Jeannine's mother was also an oral historian of the HBNS. Her neighbor, John Polk, was born to one of the first families in Swarthmore—he taught her the importance of preserving neighborhood history. Jeannine picked up the practice from her mother, and as a child, would listen to adults when they talked and later weave their tales into stories. Her work turned to preservation out of necessity, as she grew older and the elders in the neighborhood started dying, and she realized the history was in danger of being lost.

The neighborhood was always close-knit. Everyone knew and supported one another, and would come together for regular gatherings, the most important being the annual July Fourth block party. In the past ten years, the neighborhood has started to change. White families have started to move in, usually unaware of the neighborhood's history. Beginning with her next-door neighbor, she started asking the new residents if they knew they'd moved into a historically black neighborhood. Most of them didn't.

Recently, the established residents decided to hold a potluck to welcome the newcomers to the neighborhood. The event also served as a tutorial on the neighborhood's history. The elders came and spoke, as well as a historian at Swarthmore College who has researched and presented on the history of the area. The established residents noticed a split occur, between them and the newer residents, who mostly live on Union Avenue, on the east side of the neighborhood.

"We always did things as a community," Jeannine says. "Even if you didn't want to, you had to, 'cause all you had was each other."

After the potluck, the Union Avenue residents started hosting events but not inviting the black residents, even Jeannine's mother, who also lived on Union. "It's not like anybody's obligated," she says, her voice growing strained, as she tells me that they held a going-away party for another neighborhood family, who I knew growing up. They were white. She mentions a neighborhood email list that included everyone but the black families.

"I don't know if they noticed it or not, and it's not like anybody's obligated," she rationalizes. "But it is hard, when you're in the middle of being displaced, to create relationships with people who are displacing you." She hasn't figured out how to exist in this new, changing community, but she's committed to forging bonds with her neighbors nonetheless.

Back in the day, she says, her mom would welcome new neighbors with a plate of food. Today, because of dietary restrictions, she brings them flowers instead. After her mother died, she brought flowers to her house's new residents. She wrote them a letter telling them about all the memories that took place there. She did the same for the new owners of her uncle's home, which was stolen by a bank. That family responded, the others didn't.

She points out of her back window to the square on Kenyon Avenue. Amid the green lawns, a black wrought-iron fence segments one house from the others. When white folks started moving in, she says, they started erecting fences around their houses. "We grew up where the whole neighborhood was your backyard and you just ran everywhere." It's made a big difference in the character of the neighborhood.

The changes have compelled a new urgency in Jeannine's work. Her mission was always to preserve their history for the future, but now she sees it as her job to educate the people who are currently moving in. "I feel like we're Hawaii or something," she says, chuckling softly, then begins to cry. "There's a deep, deep pain."

She looks out of her back window again. "Robbie was one of the most delightful people I've ever known: kind, generous, hilarious, old school." He shared a birthday with her mother, and ever since he was a little boy, he would come to her house on that day every year until he died. She remembers how he'd come up to the back door, enticed by the smell of vegan food cooking on the stove. "I still look out this window wishing . . ." She trails off.

At the end of our conversation, she walks me out to the curb. When I tell her that I'm pregnant, she embraces me. We pose for a selfie in front of her house. Later, she shows me the spot, two doors down, where the last block party was held. After Robbie's murder, they stopped holding them. It was too painful. I imagine the gray sky cerulean, tables and barbecue grills where she gestures elegantly, and Robbie presiding over the festivities, stopping to chat with the elders, sharing a joke with his friends. "It was the most amazing and fun day," Jeannine tells me. Robbie's face lit up with his huge joker smile, his laughter crackling like fireworks.

THE SUBURBAN STRATEGY

On November 7, 2020, I made my way to the Pennsylvania Convention Center in Philadelphia. Officials had been counting ballots inside this stiflingly generic building for days, and now protesters and counterprotesters stood (and danced) outside, all within view of TV cameras. There were roughly a dozen sad-looking Trump supporters clad in red, white, and blue. About seventy Biden supporters encircled them, packed elbow to elbow, the two groups separated by police barricades, several officers, and news crews.

Cycling through the city that day, I heard many, many cheers about Trump's defeat but far fewer chants of "Biden!" This was not a moment of optimism and political triumph; it was one of catharsis. The bad guy was gone, and all we could hope was that things would go back to the way they were before. Given the personality cult that formed around Barack Obama, masking his worst policies, perhaps it's a good thing that no one likes Joe Biden that much.

In the following days, a more complete—and more complicated—picture of the election started to emerge. Against the proclamations that black people—black women, in particular—had "saved" Biden's campaign sat the countervailing information that Trump had actually gained in black and Latino communities. In Philadelphia, too, the picture was somber. In 2016, 83 percent of the city's vote went to Hillary Clinton, to Trump's 15 percent. In 2020, Trump improved his performance slightly, earning 18 percent to Biden's 81 percent. This small but not insignificant shift has led to a host of speculation. It's even more difficult to understand given Trump's disastrous handling of the COVID-19 crisis, which disproportionally harmed black and Latino communities.

Democratic voter turnout was low in the distressed urban core precincts of Philadelphia, as in other cities across Pennsylvania. By contrast, Biden drew large numbers in the suburbs, which eventually allowed him to win the state. In four suburban counties outside of Philadelphia—Bucks, Chester, Montgomery, and Delaware—he posted the highest gains of all. Here, Biden defeated Trump by 293,094 votes, whereas Clinton won by 188,353 votes in 2016. This data suggests a shift in the state's Democratic voting coalition. If in 2016 Clinton depended on large turnout in urban areas and among people of color, Biden's coalition is more suburban, whiter, and more affluent.

In many ways, Joe Biden resembles the type of suburban, middle-class white voter that shifted to him in droves in 2020. (In Delaware County he was favored more heavily than even

Barack Obama in 2008 and 2012.) And it's no wonder: Delaware County borders Wilmington, Delaware, and Biden even shares the same distinctive local accent. His political record is studded with the types of moderate achievements that could entice a former Romney or Reagan voter. Biden's focus on anti-crime legislation, in the form of the Comprehensive Crime Control Act of 1984 and the Violent Crime Control and Law Enforcement Act of 1994; on anti-gay legislation in the 1996 Defense of Marriage Act; and his opposition to desegregation in the 1970s were all policies that have shaped American cities into the segregated, policed, repressive places we know today.

Throughout his career, Biden has walked a fine line, paying lip service to minority communities and inflating his civil rights record while, in the same breath, legislating decisively against them. This careful dance has won him a fifty-year tenure in national politics and the votes of moderates, liberals, and progressives alike. Now that he's president, Biden is likely to project his politics of the suburbs across the country. It's important to understand exactly what that means: who will prosper and, more important, who will suffer.

A SEGREGATED UTOPIA

Delaware County is where I spent the first eighteen years of my life. My parents—a South African mother and Trinidadian American father, both graduates of the University of Pennsylvania—purchased our first home in the 1990s in Yeadon, a black town adjacent to the neighborhood of West Philadelphia. Yeadon was quiet and friendly, with small, conjoined houses and occasional colonial mansions where a sliver of upper-class families lived. A Tudor village stood in the center of town, housing a pizzeria, a post office, and assorted mom-and-pop shops, many of them black-owned. When I was in third grade we moved to Swarthmore, only twenty minutes southwest of Yeadon but a world away. Nothing could have prepared me for the culture shock we would experience there. As one of the few immigrant families and even fewer black families in the area, we lived a strange, isolated existence. Though the Historically Black Neighborhood of Swarthmore was established before the town itself, by African Americans who landed there during the Great Migration, Swarthmore was overwhelmingly white.

Segregation was officially abolished in Swarthmore schools in 1939, but to date I have seen no evidence that the de facto segregation of housing has ended. Today, the town is roughly 74 percent white, with African Americans making up a tiny 6 percent of the population. (Yeadon's demographics are basically the opposite: 90 percent black and with a median income of roughly $54,000, half of Swarthmore's.)

Race was at once visible and invisible in Swarthmore. There were rules governing how and where black people could live, but the existence of racism itself was denied. I can't count how many times I was told what black people could do (sports, dancing, hanging out) and what we couldn't (live in white areas, perform well in school, sing opera).

The city of Chester, located only four miles from Swarthmore, most powerfully illustrates the kind of racial inequality endemic in Delaware County. Like other black enclaves near Swarthmore, Chester today suffers from a lack of resources, but on a supercharged scale. The city is roughly 69 percent black, 21 percent white, and 12 percent Latino. The median income is just over $32,000, and roughly one-third of its residents live in poverty. Its 2019 crime rate was roughly fourteen times the national average: fifty-seven per one thousand residents were the victims of crime. In 2018, Chester was number two on NeighborhoodScout's "Murder Capitals of America" list, behind East St. Louis.

In late 2018 a photo circulated on social media of two students from the Wallingford-Swarthmore School District in white KKK-style hoods. This came shortly after letters were delivered to four Swarthmore homes voicing support for President Trump and telling the minority residents who lived there that they had to leave their homes. In 2020 a video circulated featuring two WSSD high school students who made direct racist threats and used the n-word. Rather than shock, these incidents triggered in me a sense of startling familiarity: Casual, almost playful expressions of racism marked my childhood in Delaware County. They rarely occasioned anything more than light disciplinary action. Indeed, they were often dismissed as instances of youthful indiscretion, while those of us who had been targeted were labeled as "overly sensitive." Part of me was glad that these actions had been covered in the media. That they'd been called out represented some form of progress.

FROM THE PTA TO POLITICS

As Swarthmore was grappling with these incidents, Delaware County was experiencing a more recognizable sort of progress. In January 2018, the Pennsylvania Supreme Court declared that the state's congressional district map had been gerrymandered by Republicans. This resulted in districts that were comically illogical. Delaware County was part of the infamous "Goofy Kicking Donald Duck" district—the map had two separate areas that resemble the cartoon characters connected by a thin sliver. The map was redrawn just in time for the 2018 midterm elections, which saw four women elected to Congress, the largest number ever for Pennsylvania, including Mary Gay Scanlon (a former member of the Wallingford-Swarthmore School District board) and Chrissy Houlahan, who, respectively, won in Delaware County and Chester County, formerly part of reliably red districts.

Joe Biden netted nearly the same vote margin as these Democratic candidates in each of their corresponding districts. Lara Putnam, professor of history at the University of Pittsburgh, specifically identified counties like Delaware as the epicenter of the movement in 2020. These are counties with higher rates of education and economic development—and thus attractive to increasing numbers of young and mid-career professionals—and they have traditionally been dominated by moderate or "country club" Republicans. In 2016 these counties swung away from Trump. After his election, they became ground zero for new organizing by community insiders who were, until then, uninvolved in politics. Putnam's recent work has focused on grassroots pro–Democratic Party groups, like local chapters of Indivisible, that sprung up in the wake of Donald Trump's 2016 victory.

"These were the women who were librarians and ran the PTO and organized fundraisers for the girls swim team, but politics was not their focus," Putnam told me. "In place after place, literally thousands of women, usually in their fifties to seventies, took their lifetime of accumulated organizing skills, their pretty huge personal networks of connections, and not inconsiderable disposable income and poured them into rebuilding Democratic politics in places that often had little to no organized Democratic presence." Putnam believes that these trends are likely to hold in coming years: "It's not just about people shifting their vote, it's about changes in the structural-organizational landscape." By contrast, she points out that voter turnout was low in core urban precincts across the state. In majority black neighborhoods in Philadelphia, there was in fact a roughly two-point swing toward Donald Trump. In Latino neighborhoods, about seven to twelve points.

Democratic registration efforts decreased heavily during the spring and summer of 2020, as the pandemic took hold and Biden's campaign decided to forgo in-person canvassing. Furthermore, in Pennsylvania, voters can be removed from the rolls if they fail to vote during a period of five years. "People who had registered and voted in 2008 for Barack Obama and had not since voted needed to have their registration updated," Putnam told me. Voter registration had climbed in 2008, creating the most economically and racially diverse electorate in history, with the highest black voter turnout rate ever. It's easy to imagine how voter outreach targeting these groups—even if conducted remotely—might have replicated 2008's success. The fact that vote shares decreased among these communities is evidence of the Biden campaign's obliviousness toward black and working-class voters.

This lack of attention could have dire consequences. I spoke with Nikil Saval, who was elected in 2020 to the Pennsylvania State Senate as a Democrat, representing Center City, South Philadelphia, and parts of North Philadelphia. His constituency includes large black and working-class communities, the very same that saw depressed turnout in the 2020 election. For him, the problems created by racial inequality and segregation (particularly around schools) remain a key priority. The needs of his constituents are not being met around stagnating wages, drug dependency, and mass incarceration. (At the time of writing, Philadelphia has the highest incarceration rate of any major US city.) He wants to see major investments in public and social housing and an actual commitment to issues raised by the uprisings of 2020. But, as a local politician, he will need the support of the federal government to achieve these goals. He found the shifts in voting patterns in 2020 significant, and he worries they will portend fewer resources being apportioned to communities like his. "This is the entire issue," he told me.

I also reached out to Congresswoman Scanlon's office to inquire about how she plans to address issues of racial inequality in Delaware County. Her spokesperson sent back a fairly long list of sponsored legislation that addresses criminal justice, black maternal mortality, SNAP benefit expansion, and protections against eviction and bankruptcy discrimination. None of the policies addressed affordable housing, school zoning, college tuition, or climate justice—which fundamentally shaped the structural inequities I witnessed in my childhood. This is what a Democratic Party of the suburbs looks like.

WATCH YOUR BACK

At first glance, Biden's performance with black voters may seem of a piece with the overall sloppiness of his 2020 campaign. He was consistently outraised by his Democratic primary opponents, outperformed in debates, and outthought when it came to policy proposals. This explanation would comport with the bumbling yet benevolent image of "Uncle Joe" that has stuck to him since his days as Obama's vice president.

But for a politician as successful as Biden, it seems unfair—and more important, unwise—to attribute this inattention to simple oversight. He has long managed to maneuver support from black voters while pushing policies that harm the community. At the same time that he rode to victory on black votes in Delaware, he promoted policies (such as the aforementioned anti-crime legislation, as well as the Bankruptcy Abuse Prevention and Consumer Protection Act of 2005) that have had a disproportionate impact on black communities.

In the wake of his election, Biden openly thanked black voters for saving his campaign: "The African American community stood up again for me. You've always had my back, and I'll have yours." His simultaneous courting and betrayal of black voters fits neatly with the strategy he's employed successfully for the past fifty years. It should be noted that Biden is far from the only Democratic politician to triangulate with black voters and racist whites. Beginning with Bill Clinton in 1992, this version of the Southern strategy has been employed in some shape or form in every Democratic race since. Few, however, have turned it into an art form the way Biden has.

These are the same tactics I observed in Delaware County, which promoted its image as a liberal haven despite its rigidly hierarchized and segregated society, where a community like Swarthmore can flourish right next to one like Chester, the entire pipe dream marketed to potential buyers as an idyllic suburban paradise. The kind of place one could raise kids in. “Ours is a community that prides itself on being respectful and inclusive. These incidents were in direct conflict with those values,” said Wallingford-Swarthmore School District superintendent Lisa Palmer, referring to the racist incidents at the end of 2018.

The only thing left is to fight for the full actualization of working-class and poor communities of color. I believe the solution might look something like Nikil Saval’s victory. “My hope is to build a system that caters to working people’s needs,” he told me. “I work within the Democratic Party—my goal is not to serve [the party], but the people.”

It is necessary to remain steadfastly critical of political parties, especially the ones we sometimes choose to vote for. Blind support for the president or his party only affirms consent for the administration and encourages apathy among a public that should remain vigilant. Biden and the Democratic Party, after all, have given us no reason to trust them.

HOME GOING

The word *home*, for me, carries only anxiety and dissonance. So many of my memories take place in airports and car rides, in faraway states and distant countries. My mind is a catalog of differing landscapes: the parched, yellowing grass of a Johannesburg winter; Philadelphia row houses packed with South African families; the lush jungle heat of Trinidad.

In Swarthmore, my small, liberal white hometown, their friendliness toward me was like the thin layer of ice that grew over Crum Creek every winter—it was easy enough to see the dark current rushing underneath. The racism was everywhere, just silent enough to not be noticed. But I was the right kind of black person: overachieving, eager to please, light-skinned. My parents refused to plant roots in that town. The racism wasn't as bad as where and when they came from, so we sucked it up. We lived in a standoff with it for twelve years.

My great-grandmother's two-story brick twin in St. Albans,

Queens, with a nice black family next door. Fresh buljol and bake straight out of the oven; rice and peas and turkey on Thanksgiving. Six hours in traffic from Philadelphia to New York; watching the fog break over the Verrazano at lunchtime; mothballs and Epsom salts and my grandmother banging "How Great Thou Art!" on her stand-up piano. Sunflowers twice my height, their faces bigger than my father's. Cucumbers longer than my arm, eggplants, peppers, all grown from her back garden.

You are my home, the man who will be my husband coos to me as we lie wrapped around each other in bed, one week into our acquaintance. *I am your home*, I assure him. We are each other's shield, refuge, sanctuary.

"A good deal about California does not, on its own preferred terms, add up," said Joan Didion of her home state. California confused and disquieted her. By her own admission, she could never quite figure it out. I'd argue that it has nothing to do with California itself—any place filled with humans, contradictory beings by nature, will also carry their contradictions. For Wanda Coleman, California was another yoke—like her race, gender, and poverty—that she had to struggle against. California is a place like any other, full of joys and injustices and mundanities, where people fight to live every day. Such is the nature of one's home.

The California of my youth is sun-bleached, overexposed. The strange comfort of my father's best friend's house in Orange County. For the first time, no white people at all, only blacks, Latinos, and Asians. The manic, sugarcoated thrill of Disneyland. San Francisco, viewed from afar, under a thick blanket of fog. Feeling the ground shake, alone, in the living room of my grandfather's apartment.

I was always suspicious of California negroes, so carefree and unencumbered by the brutality of the East, with its slave-built institutions, its plantations, its castes. The land was so beautiful, the possibilities so open. We East Coasters had earned our grit, I thought. Those Californians had the nerve to exercise outdoors, to smile, to date interracially. It was too fanciful for me, I thought. I'd never live there.

On a Wednesday night in 1969, my grandmother Sue called my father into the kitchen of their apartment in Rochdale, Queens. "I'm leaving your dad on Friday," she told him. "You can come with me or you can stay, I'll leave it up to you." My grandfather had hit her. It only happened once, but it was the last of many injuries. She bought a gun and had planned to use it on him. She thought better of it and decided she would leave instead.

Sue and my grandfather both worked the night shift and rarely saw my father. When she approached him in the kitchen, my father had no idea their marriage was on the rocks. She was determined to go to California, and she would let him, eleven years old at the time, choose if he would stay in New York with his increasingly volatile father or leave everything he'd ever known. Two days later, his baby sister in tow, they slipped out of New York, my grandfather none the wiser, and drove across the US to California, with my father navigating from the passenger's seat.

Sue was never the typical grandmother. I barely knew her growing up because she was living in Japan with her second husband, a kind, educated white man named Ed. When they met, they foreswore anything that would tie them down, including owning possessions and having children, and traveled the world for forty years together, through Iran, Saudi Arabia, France, and eventually landing in Japan. In her seventies, having left Japan for Los Angeles, she signed with an agent and took up work as a movie extra. "I'll pose nude if they want me to," she'd say often.

The only time I can remember seeing my grandparents together was at my college graduation. They spent the whole weekend at separate hotels and at opposite ends of the table. At the close of the weekend, my family idled in two separate cars, waiting to say goodbye before taking off. My grandfather took the front car, my grandmother the back. "Go say goodbye!" my mother vented, elbowing my grandfather toward the door. He shuffled to the other car, sulking like a chastened schoolboy. "Bye, Sue," he muttered through the window. That was the last time they ever spoke.

When I ask my grandmother about why she chose California, she tells me, in her own way, that she knew they'd find a better life there. From the pioneers to black defense industry workers, opportunity has always drawn Americans to its left quarter.

Most Americans think of the Great Migration as the period between 1916 and 1940 when roughly 1.5 million black Americans moved from the south to northern cities, in search of greater economic opportunity and to escape racial persecution in the Jim Crow South. However, historians recognize that event as only the first—and smaller—of two waves of migration that took place in the twentieth century. The second—which historians termed the Second Great Migration—took place between 1941 and the late 1970s and encompassed roughly five million black Americans who moved from rural areas to urban centers in the South, North, and West. In "The Second Great Migration: An Historical Overview," James N. Gregory writes:

> Within one generation, a people who had been mostly rural became mostly urban. A people mostly southern spread to all regions of the United States. A people mostly accustomed to poverty and equipped with farm skills now pushed their way into the core of the American economy. And other changes followed. A people who had lacked access to political rights and political influence now gained both.

The Great Migration represented nothing less than a complete reshaping of black identity in the US, one that granted them economic opportunities and political influence that persist to this day.

At the end of World War II, a booming defense industry drew black Americans to Los Angeles. This influx saw the black population grow from 63,700 in 1940 to a staggering 763,000 in 1970.

When my grandmother reflects on the idea, indistinct but

ever-present, of opportunity drawing her to California, these changing demographics are undoubtedly one factor. Before she left, my grandfather told my grandmother that he wanted to go there, and even years after they divorced he would tell her, "I would have moved to California for you."

"I just didn't want to move there with *you*," she would reply. All around them back then, leaving was in the air, and the West beckoned, more than ever before, to people like them.

Born in Kansas City, Kansas, in 1926, my grandfather, Michael Sr., was an intelligent man born with a restless spirit. He and my father, his namesake, couldn't be less alike. My father is mild-mannered, respectful, patient almost to a fault, he clearly made himself everything his father wasn't.

When he was sixteen, Michael Sr. falsified his age to join the navy and was sent to World War II. He was injured during his enlistment and a metal plate was used to patch his skull. Years ago, an aunt told me his erratic behavior was due to that brain injury. For the most part, my family resists these sorts of retrospective readings. He was who he was, they tell me. After the navy, he worked as a waiter on the Santa Fe railroad and, after my father was born, as a captain's steward on a cruise ship. Henceforth until he retired in his eighties, he hauled passengers' luggage as a skycap, first for TWA and then for American Airlines, when the company was sold.

My grandmother worked as an operator for the telephone company. My grandfather's job, consisting of physically demanding menial labor, was a good, steady job for a black man in those days, guaranteeing him benefits and free flights. Though he was uneducated, he was intelligent and worldly. He was well traveled due to his service in the navy, on trains and cruise ships. Every day, he bought a copy of *The New York Times* at the airport and read it front to back. He met my grandmother at an NAACP dinner in Queens. Both of them were well read and dreamed of better lives, lives out of reach for black people of their era.

After they married, Sue and Michael Sr. settled in Queens near my great-grandmother, in Rochdale Village, a sprawling superblock cooperative development built in 1963, replete with a public park, schools, and churches. Built amid the unrest of the Civil Rights Movement, Rochdale was imagined as a model of racial harmony, where families of all colors could live peacefully alongside one another. In reality, the number of black families was heavily restricted, and 80 percent of Rochdale's families were white. The surrounding neighborhood of St. Albans, in contrast, was almost entirely black.

My father remembers being chased out of public spaces by Rochdale's security guards, who rode around in Cushman buggies they deemed "roach coaches." My father was friends with people of all races; many of his friends were Jewish, including one friend that he played chess with by mail. In each letter, they would play one move, and the game lasted for years.

My grandmother repeats the stories of her marriage to me often, as if she is entering them into the record of some make-believe courtroom. Or maybe she always knew I would write about them. There was the Brazilian singer she learned of through my grandfather's cousin, who showed her the woman's photo after they'd broken up. There was the possible love child somewhere in the Midwest. There was the first time he took her to Kansas City shortly after they were married, when my grandfather left her in his apartment for what he told her was an errand. She started menstruating, and with no car or money, she sat there for hours bleeding on the couch, waiting for him to return. When their friends showed up bearing sanitary napkins, they told her my grandfather was with another woman.

My grandma Sue was born Agnes Boyce in 1932 in the countryside of Trinidad, in the town of Arima. She grew up in her grandparents' one-room house with her aunts, uncles, and cousins. Her grandfather was a short, ill-tempered man, partial to rum and outbursts of violence against his wife and family. Her father was a Chinese man my great-grandmother met briefly in Trinidad. The whole affair is shrouded in mystery. They've never called it rape, but it's clear that what happened wasn't invited, and after Sue was born, he was never around. She hated the name Agnes and changed it to Sue as an adult, in part to honor her Asian heritage. I've always found it curious that she would want to honor that side of her family, but grew to see it as part of her love of the exotic, of wanderlust. She always seemed to accept the absence of her father and whoever he might have been. I never heard her call him "father." In her twenties, she worked in a duty-free department store catering to cruise ship passengers in Port of Spain. My great-grandparents had settled in the United States in the mid-1950s, and my grandmother traveled there for a short visit and never left.

Daisy, called Ena, my great-grandmother. A strong, stocky, mahogany-skinned woman. Pious. She wore skirts to her ankles every day, never pants or anything shorter, because that's what the Lord wanted. After the Chinese man she found my great-grandfather Leslie, a gentle giant from Barbados. A loyal servant of the Lord and her church, Seventh-day Adventists. From sundown Friday to sundown Saturday was the Sabbath, which meant no TV, dancing, or music, except gospel. Every Saturday for decades, Ena drove herself to Riker's Island to minister to the prisoners. She received a key to the city for her service, and once, Sue tells me, a man stopped them on the street to thank her for changing his life. When she moved to the States, Ena worked first as a maid and then as a practical nurse at Creedmoor Psychiatric Center. Eventually, Ena and Leslie saved enough to buy the twin house in St. Albans. It had three small bedrooms upstairs and a semifinished basement, where generations of friends and family landed in the course of immigrating to the United States.

In her twenties, Sue entered a beauty pageant in Harlem and after that did some modeling, until she was offered a lingerie shoot. Ena forbade her, and that was the end of her career. After decades of world travel with her second husband, Sue moved back to Los Angles with Ed. Until she was in her eighties, she worked as a guide on a tour bus in Beverly Hills, spinning tales of old Hollywood legends for foreigners and hobbyists. If fate had unfolded slightly differently, she would have been a working actor—perhaps even a star—but in the absence of that, she performed in her everyday life. She keeps their rent-controlled one-bedroom in Brentwood spotless, her hair slicked back with Vaseline, her outfits dapper and always matching. She brings elegance to everything she does. And nearly every time I see her, she finds a way to tell me she is content: grateful to have been liberated from a bad marriage, grateful for her life with Ed, and happy, nearly every day of her life.

In retrospect, read against the stories of my forebears, perhaps it seems obvious that I would fall in love with someone for whom home is also a palimpsest. If you had heard the story of my life and then met him, you'd have picked him right away from the pack of charming misfits that populate my romantic history. At least you would have thought I'd recognize it when he sat across from me.

We first meet in the vestibule of the white-columned hall of the artist residency, where we gather in the evening for meals and linger around the fire, sipping whiskey and telling ghost stories. I'm on my way out the door, zipping up my full-length parka, harried, typically brusque. He greets me with a full smile and an enthusiastic "Hello!" He wears a sleek leather jacket and boots, completely underdressed for a New Hampshire spring, which has delivered three feet of fresh snow to our temporary doorstep.

Who is *this guy?* I think. Whispers follow him around the colony's campus, from his origins to his bibliography (substantial for his age) to his dashing looks. I remain skeptical when he tells me he's an architect's son from Dubai. *Another rich kid*, I think, and shrug him off, until dinner a couple nights later when I find myself seated across the table from him.

I find out that his palimpsest resembles mine but is even more unrooted. Parents from Iran and Italy, a childhood in the Venice countryside, then many years in Abu Dhabi. It turns out he is the opposite of a rich kid: His father is an unsuccessful architect, and they struggled with money his whole life. Smart and practical, he worked his way through college in England and settled in London, where the early part of his adult life played out much like mine in New York: graduate school, publishing, networking, working oneself determinedly up the ladder of success.

He's lived in Morocco, India, and lastly South Africa, drawn there by the dream of a post-independence multiracial utopia. After a year in a coloured section of Cape Town, he found that to be a lie, just like all the other lies countries tell about themselves. We find out we were both there at the same time in 2013, both partook in the spontaneous mourning and festivities when Mandela passed away. A few days after we meet, he sends me Robert F. Kennedy's "Day of Affirmation" speech, delivered at the University of Cape Town in 1966:

> I come here this evening because of my deep interest and affection for a land settled by the Dutch in the mid-seventeenth century, then taken over by the British, and at last independent; a land in which the native inhabitants were at first subdued, but relations with whom remain a problem to this day; a land which defined itself on a hostile frontier; a land which has tamed rich natural

> resources through the energetic application of modern technology; a land which was once the importer of slaves, and now must struggle to wipe out the last traces of that former bondage. I refer, of course, to the United States of America.

I wait outside the door to his room. I work up the courage to ask what's happening between us, and it turns out we both feel the same way. We hold a public reading together in the cabin James Baldwin once wrote in, and hours after everyone has gone to bed, he sits in front of me and takes my hands in his. In the early hours of the morning, we kiss for the first time as the snow blankets our footfalls. From this moment on, we are inseparable.

Almost immediately, he disclaims all the most difficult items from his past, "So you know what you're getting into," he tells me. A physical disability, bad relationships, addiction. A family marred by violence, mental illness, displacement. Parents who are now close to destitute, so racked by shame and guilt that they've stopped calling him.

When he departs the artist colony two weeks before I do, he decamps to another residency in upstate New York. The place lies in the countryside outside a small weather-beaten city on the Hudson River, a former whaling village now teeming with artists who have also been defeated by the city. This is where our future begins to take shape.

In my twenties, I made what was possible to make of a home in New York City. In a smaller, more practical place, this would have meant one apartment, perhaps even a mortgage. A single neighborhood, a stable set of friends, a salary. In New York, it meant increasingly smaller apartments and no savings. He is similarly purged from London, so we scour the map, looking for places we can afford that won't bore us to death.

In the city on the river, winter begins to thaw and we pass long evenings being sung to by the crickets in the green outdoors. In a bookstore café, surrounded by used paperbacks, he confesses to me, "I'm never going to make a lot of money," like I am some unwilling priest. Some years ago, along with the decision to become a writer, I foreclosed any idea of financial security. I couldn't commit myself to my art and to money at the same time. I know that my life will look different than the one my parents wished for me, and as long as I can do what I want, I'm happy with that. But even so, as I laugh off his concern, I see the water rushing in over our heads.

Cut off from friends and familiar surroundings, he grows resentful, angry. In London, he was a rising star in the literary scene, but in America, he's just another foreigner with a Muslim last name. We can't afford a lawyer to apply for a visa, so instead he leaves the country every six months in accordance with his visa waiver. Every time he returns to the US, he's flagged for further questioning at passport control, and I walk him to the crowded back room filled with other brown-skinned people before I'm made to leave. Hours later, we hug tearfully in baggage claim, and he refuses to disclose the finer details of what happened there.

We fight mercilessly. Call it adjustment or the rot seeping in all around us. Over time, my hot temper turns to rage. His mental illness deepens with circumstance. We can't afford therapy, so we become enemies as much as lovers. During one fight, I pull every picture from every wall in our house and punch a hole in a door. We argue on car rides, spend nights in separate bedrooms and hotel rooms. We sometimes argue for days and make up for days. But our conversations never lag, and we never grow tired of each other's company. We get married. We make love almost every night, and we spend every day, in some form, together.

Michael Sr. dies in 2015, and my husband and I go to California together for the first time. In a small funeral home in South Los Angeles, I learn that my grandfather enlisted at the beginning of World War II with the dream of being a deep-sea diver, but at that time black soldiers weren't allowed to take on these roles. Instead, he worked the mess hall on a navy ship, and even though he hated the work and having to watch white soldiers live his dream, he finished his service. Soon after my father tells this story, two Asian soldiers, possibly not older than twenty-one, take their places in the front of the room and fold his flag. His portrait, a ninety-year-old man in his WORLD WAR II VETERAN baseball cap, his eyes wide and confused, stares back at us from an enlarged photo that is next to a modest floral arrangement. Aside from my aunt, my father, and my husband, I know no one else here, and as I look around, I realize I have never been at a funeral so sparsely attended.

A woman I've never seen before takes the podium to give

some tearful remarks about my grandfather. She is curvy and beautiful, a classic black bombshell, perhaps forty-five, with caramel skin, her hair swept back neatly, a large hat covering most of her face. She wears a skintight black pencil dress that reaches to her knees, a scoop neck with cleavage hoisted up to ten.

The repast is held at my grandfather's favorite bar, a dark club in an anonymous strip mall that my grandfather frequented every day until he got sick. His friends are old players—septuagenarians in fedoras and guayaberas who hunch over the bar and occasionally slide over to the dance floor to two-step. My grandfather's favorite stool is left empty as we sip his favorite brand of Merlot. The bombshell drifts in an hour late with a younger woman by her side. She chats with the old players before making her way to me and tells me urgently how much my grandfather meant to her. Finally, she coos, "He always let me use the pool at his apartment complex. Maybe I could come by every once in a while for a swim?"

A few months after they'd left, back in 1970, Michael Sr. found Sue's phone number in California. He called and harassed them frequently until he finally made the move to Los Angeles to be near his children. The tussles of divorce began, and my father and his sister got caught in the middle. It got so bad that my father began dreading speaking to his father. Their relationship only began to repair when my father joined the golf team in the ninth grade. Michael Sr. developed an interest in the sport and, every week, took my father to his golf lesson. They never talked about the divorce or their feelings, but on the golf course they were finally able to be around each other with some measure of peace. Michael Sr. remained an avid golfer his entire life; most of my memories of him are at putt-putt and on the driving range.

Though my grandfather kept the same job in Los Angeles as a baggage handler, his situation dramatically improved there. His job required him to work primarily outdoors, meeting travelers outside the airport and ferrying their luggage into the building. He had to brave the cold of New York City winters, dressing in thermal underwear and fighting through snow to arrive at work. There were no such obstacles in Los Angeles. He moved on, bought himself a one-bedroom condo a few minutes up the road from the Los Angeles airport in Culver City. Every day, he ate his meals at the Jewish deli down the road and drank with his friends at the bar. I never had a conversation with my grandfather close enough for him to disclose his feelings. I have no idea if he was happy. Content, maybe. He was free—of my grandmother, of a certain set of expectations. I suspect that was enough for him.

In early 2015, my grandfather's apartment has been empty for a few months. I am working as a barista and an office assistant while my husband translates books for a few hundred dollars each. We realize we have run out of road in the East. There are no other jobs to be had in the city on the river. My husband and I find publishers for our first books. Soon, a part-time teaching job in Los Angeles presents itself. I realize that being so far away from my home will almost put us on an equal footing. My husband makes his case. I recognize this as a fresh start.

We pack everything we can into our hatchback car, the rest we leave in the front yard for passersby. The morning we set out for the West Coast, it's all still sitting there, the only vestiges of our permanence, waiting for some new person or to die waterlogged in the snow, as if the life we made here never existed.

We head south first, through Washington, DC, to visit friends, and then to Georgia. When we hit the highway west of Atlanta, we're into new territory. I've never been to the Deep South before. We double back to Nashville, then down through Tennessee's rolling green hills. We end up in Tupelo, Mississippi, at an old burger joint frequented by Elvis. We sit in a booth next to a picture of the King and eat fried green beans. Everyone else is white and seems to know one another. When the waitress comes our way, we brace ourselves for cruelty or dismissal, but she's sweet as can be and tells us what to see on our visit, much friendlier than they are up north. We leave the place relieved and full, and from the highway on the way back to our motel we see a sign for a pecan stand named after David Duke.

The road gets more deserted, the land bigger, drier. We eat at truck stops and visit roadside attractions: car henge, Route 66, Technicolor-painted canyons. We sleep in fleabags and watch our car, which houses all our earthly belongings, from the window. The prairie turns to desert and our map takes us down a dirt road, for which our hatchback is woefully unfit. I clutch the lamps in the back seat to keep them from breaking. Then the desert turns to highway and we're facing a canyon of a million yellow lights and we're here, hello, Los Angeles.

. . .

We are reborn in California: excited to be in a city again, lulled by sunshine, giddy on marijuana. My husband drives my grandfather's 1985 Mercedes around the streets of Los Angeles, smoke billowing from the driver's-side window. We nickname the car the Pimpmobile, in honor of Mike Sr. A few years on from his death, stories about who he really was start leaking out. We learn that, while my father and aunt were cleaning out the apartment, they found empty condom wrappers littering the floor behind my grandfather's bed. My aunt tells me about one time when she called him a few years before he died. "What're you up to, Dad?" she asked. "Smoking reefers," he barked from the other line, "don't tell no one!"

We sometimes joke that we feel like country mice let loose in the city. We're grateful for every party invite, elated by bad poetry readings, taken with the novelty of food delivery: anything we want to eat, at any time of day. In the Hudson Valley, we bought much of our food from farms and cooked it all from scratch. My husband falls in love with the place instantly. The weather and the vibe fit him to a T. He spends hours exploring old neighborhoods no one else cares to visit and searching through historical archives.

Culver City was founded as a sundown town in 1917, with ads promoting it as a "model little white city." Today it's integrated and gentrified, dominated by the kind of yuppie stroller set you find in Los Feliz and Park Slope, Brooklyn. My grandfather's apartment has a balcony that overlooks Jefferson Boulevard, one of Southwest LA's main thoroughfares. When I was young, my grandfather's neighborhood was largely industrial (his condo complex is located on the site of a former MGM backlot). Jefferson forms the western boundary of Culver City and the eastern border of what's commonly known as South Central Los Angeles. We spot police cars on Jefferson nearly every day, and every few days a black person is stopped in their car or seated in front of a squad car on the pavement.

After witnessing several of these incidents, one evening, while sitting on the balcony, we see a car pulled over. I decide not to be a passive bystander and take out my phone and start filming. I wave to them so that they know someone is watching this encounter. The police car trains its spotlight on me and the entire apartment is lit up as the officer's voice thunders through the loudspeaker. I'm unable to sleep that night.

My father is yellow-skinned with Sue's eyes, but he is unmistakably black, with full lips and kinky hair that he wore in an Afro for much of his youth. He remembers it as a mostly peaceful time, though he tends to gloss over difficulty and discomfort. That was up until the summer of 1968, just before they moved away, after Martin Luther King Jr. was shot.

My father was pulled over by police for the first time in Los Angeles. He was about sixteen, driving his father's Mercedes-Benz to pick my aunt and her boyfriend up from school when a police car drove past them in the opposite direction, then pulled in front of them and stopped. More police cars came and then a paddy wagon—every time my father turned around, there was another one there. A black police officer approached him with his hand on his gun. My father trembled. Meanwhile, my aunt's school bus approached from behind, the schoolchildren watching as my father pulled his license and registration from the glove box and handed it to the officer. Luckily, my father is named after his own father. Had the school bus not been there, had his name not matched his father's on the registration, the scene may have played out very differently.

These types of incidents were so frequent that, one day, my grandmother stormed into the police station and demanded they stop harassing my father. The memories are as common as sunset drives and teenage parties. My father left California as suddenly as he arrived with the determination of a scorned lover, returning to the East Coast for college and never going back. He received an ROTC scholarship to attend the University of California, but instead he secured the grants and loans necessary to attend the University of Pennsylvania. He met my mother, settled in Philadelphia, and my brother and I were born.

One year into our time in California, my husband's family calls him for his birthday from Abu Dhabi on Skype. His parents impart their wishes and soon his father leaves the room. His mother lowers her voice and tells him that the money is gone. After several loans, his father had used all the money from the sale of his in-law's home to prop up his business. They wire us the couple of grand they have left and we use it to rent them an apartment in Baja California, a couple of miles from the beach.

In 2007, at age sixty-four, my husband's father spent six months in jail after money was reported missing in his office. Rather than carry out a full investigation, his father's employer decided to imprison all the senior staff until they'd discovered exactly what had happened. That was the acceleration point of their downward spiral, when my husband's mother sold every last one of their belongings to pay for a lawyer. After his college graduation, my husband moved home and got a job to support them. Eventually, they let his father out of prison after making him sign a document saying he would never sue over his wrongful incarceration. It was the kind of totalizing tragedy that is difficult for many Westerners to fathom—his father had done nothing that qualifies as illegal in the US—and that happens to ordinary people in the UAE every day.

My in-laws' shame and my husband's pain collide. They are unable to get along. As soon as we're done moving them in we leave bitterly, and a few weeks later, a family member buys them a plane ticket to Europe. My husband calls and emails, but this time they don't answer. The wind has shifted suddenly and irrevocably, and we never hear from them again.

With the realization that his family is gone, my husband falls into a deep depression. For one year, he does not work, he does not see friends or meet colleagues. He stays confined to our 650-square-foot apartment, smoking joints on the porch, watching TV and reading, while I hide from him, even though I've done nothing wrong, wondering how much of this is my fault.

I take every job I can find. I work every day. My insomnia grows worse from stress and I can barely sleep. I travel every few weeks for my book tour, and our relationship falls between the cracks. We argue with an intensity that we have never had before, and I sometimes forget why we fell in love in the first place.

The California sun has no memory. It does not allow bitterness or resentment. The law of the land is *Be nice!*, and I've always found niceness suspicious for how often it's sold as true kindness and generosity. In California, drivers will stop in the middle of a busy thoroughfare to let cars merge ahead of them. In Philadelphia, you must fight to wedge yourself into traffic. And then there are the fit, happy people who smile at you on the street. I've spent my adult life learning to avoid eye contact; how to deter ne'er-do-wells with an air of measured toughness.

I'm helplessly out of place here, always spoiling for a fight. I start arguments in line at CVS, I square out drivers on the highway, I blare at them with my horn. Part of me misses the aggression of the East Coast, while part of me is fruitlessly trying to act out the battle raging inside me.

I begin working as a temporary lecturer at different colleges around the city. It is my first time teaching undergraduates and it feels almost as natural as writing does. I'm pleased to learn that I've found the right profession for the second time in my life. I make it a point to introduce my students to the literature of their home state, which includes Joan Didion, a standby and giant of what we now call creative nonfiction.

I teach my students about Didion's ancestor, Nancy Hardin Cornwall, who trekked westward with the Donner–Reed party in 1846. When they reached the Humboldt Sink in Nevada, Cornwall in a fateful decision split with the party. The Donner–Reeds ended in infamy and Cornwall landed in Oregon. Didion's family eventually settled in Sacramento, where several generations would tend to their roots and Didion would eventually be born. The lesson is an introduction to the history of California and one of its most potent myths: that of the pioneers. This myth, among others, such as California's economic dominance and its reputation as a peaceful liberal haven, Didion sought to problematize in her writing.

It's Didion's ability to undermine—to slip a blade between the ribs—in a single sentence that has always thrilled the critic in me. Her strict economy, honed by her early years of writing and endlessly revising (under the exacting eye of Allene Talmey) tight captions for *Vogue*, thrills the editor in me.

One day, the Santa Ana winds stoke a raging fire on the Getty Center hill, threatening the mansions south of Sunset. In class, I read aloud from Didion's "Los Angeles Notebook": *I have neither heard nor read that a Santa Ana is due, but I know it, and almost everyone I have seen today knows it too. We know it because we feel it . . .*

I cut class short and shuffle quickly back to my faculty house just off campus, where we moved from Culver City after I was hired as a full-time lecturer. My husband and I arrange to collect Sue and Ed from their apartment just south of Sunset Boulevard, which marks the boundary of the current evacuation area. Once they're in our grip, we hum on pleasant nervous energy all weekend, watching the sky turn lilac at dusk, eating Taiwanese takeout from around the corner, wondering when things will return to normal. Ed wakes up first, has his coffee and studies. He is a student in a lifelong learning program at UCLA; he takes extensive notes in notebooks and in the margins of his many books. Ed and my husband have voluminous conversations about obscure historical figures and the state of humanity. My grandmother positions a chair in front of the windows of our sunroom, which look out onto the neighboring hills dotted with bungalows, Tuscan pines, and tall palm trees. She reads a romance novel and does Sudoku and dreams. The symmetry of our lives becomes apparent. Over the past year, the stability afforded by our careers has brought calm to my relationship with my husband. I realize that if all goes well, our lives will look a lot like theirs in a few decades, and I'd be perfectly happy with that.

Soon enough, the fires subside and we cart my grandparents back across town to their apartment. The air is still heavy with smoke, but they are safe. In class, we arrive at "Slouching Towards Bethlehem," and my students' quiet fascination with Didion turns to stone. For years, Didion's hippie subjects were distant historical figures to me, as foreign to a Philadelphian as the Pacific Ocean, but here they are the mothers, aunts, and neighbors of the bemused young faces staring back at me.

When we read "The White Album," the class is fascinated by Didion's renovations of form and enthralled by her proximity to the Manson Family. But then there is the issue of the protests at San Francisco State College. Late in the essay, Didion arrives on that campus soaked in ennui and finds an institution in the grips of political demonstrations that she paints as delusions. The agitations for justice she mockingly compares to an Evelyn Waugh novel and "a musical comedy about college life."

Paul is one of a handful of black students I've had since I began teaching. Proudly, he informs the class that the protest that Didion derides led to the establishment of the first ethnic studies department in the United States. Four years ago, students at this college slept in the administration building next door, their demands all too similar to those that Didion mocked in her essay. The college established an interdisciplinary Black Studies major, with professors who cycle in and out during my time here. When he's done speaking, Paul looks back down at the table, grinds his palms together. He doesn't meet my eyes and shuffles quickly out the door when the class ends.

All that weekend, I can't shake the look of disappointment on Paul's face, can't stop feeling like I'd broken the invisible contract between us. It was my duty to teach the canon, even if I didn't agree with Didion, because my students needed to be aware of her. My husband tells me, as he always does, that I shouldn't be so hard on myself. I try to write, but nothing comes.

The next week, Paul doesn't turn in his story for the workshop. I'm notified by the school that he is ill, and a few days later, I learn that he's taken his life.

Paul is the second student at our tiny college to die in the space of a single month. Both of them are black, and at a school with a population of about two thousand, they represent a statistically significant portion of the college's minuscule black population.

The college holds a community gathering with counselors and chaplains on hand where we run through grief exercises and write memories of Paul on slips of colored construction paper. It's mostly teachers who show up. I'm wrecked, but I try my best to reflect composure. The whole exercise feels pointless. Midway through the proceedings, one of Paul's friends stands up. "This college is killing us," he announces, and then leaves the room.

A couple of days later, Paul's friends organize a memorial on the main quad. Everyone wears white, and an enlarged portrait of Paul sits on an easel overlooking the quad. They wheel in a loudspeaker, pass around a microphone, and play Pop Smoke and Nipsey Hussle in between remembrances (two black men whose lives, by that point, had also been cut short). I wear a white T-shirt and my work pants. I watch his friends embrace from a bench at the back of the crowd. There are mostly students of color, myself, and a Latino administrator. Under a tree stand two campus police officers in full gear and sunglasses, arms folded across their chests, surveying the crowd.

In "Sentimental Journeys," Didion reflects accurately on the many false narratives about life in New York City and how this tendency to mythos distorted the reaction to the case of the Central Park jogger, making villains of the five black boys who would be jailed as defendants and later exonerated. "For those who proceeded from the conviction that there was under way a conspiracy to destroy blacks, particularly black boys, a belief in the innocence of these defendants, a conviction that even their own statements had been rigged against them or wrenched from them, followed logically." She presents this idea as fallacy, the imaginings of a hysterical black public when, in fact, this is exactly what happened. Didion's musings on the city and the trial have aged very well, with the glaring exception of this section, where her racism dramatically limits her analysis. This remains the most enduring and fatal criticism of her entire body of work.

I've been under the spell of Didion's sentences for years. A part of me will always love Didion. But what happens when the one you love doesn't love you back?

After five years in Los Angeles I'm summoned north for a job at the University of California. We end up not far from where Didion grew up, in a small city outside of Sacramento that I've never been to or even seen on a map, in the state's agricultural Central Valley. Every few weeks, we hear tires screeching on the I-80 and occasionally the crunch of metal. We read in the paper one morning about a road-rage incident in which a driver shot at cars in traffic. When the police arrived, he fled his vehicle, escaped from the highway, and ran through our neighborhood while the police pursued by car, helicopter, and on foot. By the time we wake up, the shelter-in-place order has been lifted.

In my mid-twenties, I began breaking out in hives spontaneously. They would appear at seemingly random times: sometimes after physical exertion, but also sometimes after sitting still. Sometimes after eating but also sometimes when I'd been sitting for a while, reading or watching television. The breakouts happen more frequently here, and they become more debilitating. My skin worsens. The rainy winter passes with no major incidents, but as the weather gets warmer and drier, the environment takes its toll on my body. I find that I can no longer eat things I could in Los Angeles. Wheat is out of the question. I can't even think about butter. And then, as winter turns to spring, I develop, for the first time, cold sores at the edges of my lips. I go through bottle after bottle of medicine, only to have them return a short while later.

What distinguished Didion is her style, so carefully milled as to be not noticed at first. It took me a few reads to really be captured by her, but when I was, she took hold. When I moved here I began to understand her, to feel her. Her sentences are somewhat flat in tone, but the excitement comes from the acuity in her observations, which accumulate over pages to assemble a full, clear picture.

Sacramento is a flat landscape where the rhythms of life mimic the crop season. The winter is wet and cold by California standards, requiring a light parka, and the summer heat—which lasts from May until October—is scorching, usually hovering in the mid to upper nineties, and consistently in the triple digits in June, July, and August. There is snow on the mountains, dense fog that blankets crops in the fall, giving life to wine-country grapes, fires in the dry season, and the occasional earthquake. Out here, you watch this cycle of violent rebirth and destruction every year, which mirrors the politicians that cycle in and out of state office in Sacramento's downtown.

In "Why I Write," Didion describes her writing process as one of capturing "pictures that shimmer": "You can't think too much about these pictures that shimmer. You just lie low and let them develop. You stay quiet. You don't talk to many people and you keep your nervous system from shorting out." I don't feel

Didion's presence right away, but as my months wear on here, slowly she develops.

Our financial situation slowly improves. We rent a brand-new townhouse, complete with stainless steel appliances, motorized blinds, and a two-car garage, for the same price as a one-bedroom apartment in Los Angeles. It's the first time I've rented a house with stairs, more space than we know what to do with. We have barely enough furniture to fill half of it; we buy a new mattress without a bed frame and sleep on the floor. We develop a taste for nice wines, which are produced in abundance and sold cheaply in the region. Oftentimes, we sit on our balcony, awestruck at our luck.

This new life chafes my husband more than me. For months after his parents left, he suffered panic attacks in grocery stores. He'd stand in the aisles overwhelmed by the Technicolor labels, the piles of Edenic produce, and the thought that his family—wherever they may be—might not be able to afford food. The knowledge that they wouldn't accept our help if offered only makes the pain even worse.

Though we weren't rich, I grew up never going without. My father is a sensible man. He's owned Honda Accords for my entire life, drives them until they stop running and then buys another. He's never bought an item of clothing over fifty dollars. My mother was a spendthrift. For her, assimilation took the form of middle-class attainment: a nice home, Coach purses, and a leased C-Class Mercedes.

Whatever success I've achieved has hung awkwardly on me. I lay these facts alongside my decision to become a writer. I consider them in the light of our ten-foot windows, try to parse them as I stare at another perfect California sunset.

Everywhere next to highways and railroad tracks, in empty parking lots and fields, you will see tarps and shopping carts piled by the side of the road, people walking about, chatting, living their everyday lives in view of drivers on their morning commutes. You will notice most of the unhoused are not white, and in fact about one-quarter of them are black, even though black people are only 7 percent of the state's population. Black California lives on freeway exits and underpasses, in tents and lean-tos. This is where the dream ends for so many of my parents' generation, who once came westward on the whisper of hope. These are the Great Migration's children.

I have always prided myself on my grit, but this place has made me realize that perhaps East Coast toughness masks a greater vulnerability. That as difficult as New York and Philadelphia are, with their towering housing projects and subway systems and social strata, those structures also protect human beings from the elements. In the Central Valley, there is only heat and wind, with no mountains or buildings to break them. In the summer, the temperature is always above one hundred; in the winter, the wind howls and shakes our townhouse. The fires rage. The earth trembles.

My body refuses to adjust, a technical result of the harsh climate and lack of humidity. But I see it as something deeper: a manifestation of the deep turbulence at the heart of this place. The California Dream is just like the American one: a total lie. But there is no paradise on earth, and for now and forever in some way, this place is my home.

FREEDOM, PT. 2

In this period when the covers camouflaging the corruption and racism of the highest political offices are rapidly falling away, when the bankruptcy of the global system of capitalism is becoming apparent, there was the possibility that more people—Black, Brown, Red, Yellow and white—might be inspired to join our growing community of struggle. Only if this happens will I consider this project to have been worthwhile.

—Angela Davis, *An Autobiography*

This story entails many different stories and the person I used to be. I was so free with my words, but now freedom denotes nothing but risk. Who I used to be fills me with deep longing and anxiety. Perhaps you are reading this out of some morbid desire for gossip: to know the who, what, where. To piece together the identities behind the pseudonyms and infer all kinds of things about all the people involved. Women's pain is always made into entertainment, our tears turned to dollars, black women especially. But I have no control over that, and it is not my intention. As I asked myself many times in the lost years described here: Why write? Why fucking bother? I almost stopped altogether because it brought me nothing but pain, but not writing brought me nothing but sadness, and then I found my answer, which is not an answer but a statement of being: This is who I am. This is me, being.

. . .

My mother was a dominating presence in my life. She was a memorable figure, completely unladylike. She said whatever was on her mind, she fought, she cursed, and she complained. She hated cleaning and hosting guests. She loved to cook, but she was proud. As we ate, she would brag about the meal the entire way through. She commanded respect from my father and never lost an argument to him, at least not in public.

In many ways, she embodied the principles of feminism. Out of sheer force of will, she demanded to be treated equally to any man. Though she never spoke of feminism, my guess is that she agreed with its tenets. Like me, she probably felt disconnected from feminism because of her race. Growing up under South African apartheid, where race explicitly dictated every detail of her life and was the difference between life and death, gender was likely a secondary concern. Early on, I internalized this thinking as well: that "feminism" as discussed by academics and pundits was something that only white women had the luxury to be concerned about.

In pictures from her youth, she was young, vibrant, thin. The mother I knew was overweight, disgruntled, isolated, sedentary. I came to realize only in adulthood that she was depressed. Till the day she died, she only called South Africa "home." My parents acknowledged that she was smarter than my father, but due to circumstances, he ended up more successful. Lost potential trailed her constantly, and it was no secret that our family and her move to America were partly to blame for that loss.

When she was young, my mother was a freedom fighter. Recently, I learned that in their green card interview, the immigration officer informed my newly married parents that her name had come up with INTERPOL. She was one of the most wanted student activists in South Africa. Though we knew some of the facts of her past, she didn't speak often about that time; instead we were left to fill in the picture from anecdotes dropped here and there in conversation. She seemed totally disconnected from her past; it was like something that had happened to someone else, somewhere else, a long time ago. She changed when she moved to the United States, became infected with the fear common to so many immigrants.

In high school, I started to rebel seriously. My political identity began to take shape, and I made friends with kids my mom deemed misfits. She reacted violently to these changes. Our fights were legendary, stretching over days, ending with a teary resolution only to pop up in some different form weeks later. We were at a permanent standoff over nearly every choice I made. Her favorite target was my appearance. From a young age, she took me to have my hair chemically straightened, as was common back then, to avoid fights over her detangling and styling my unruly hair herself. I hated going to the hairdresser and didn't care much for how it looked. I wore thrift-store clothes and band T-shirts instead of the matching sets my mother tried to foist on me. *You could be so gorgeous*, she'd tell me, *if you wore decent clothes and took care of yourself.*

In my senior year of high school, I saved my money and bought tickets to see my favorite band in an outdoor theater in

New Jersey. Afterward, my friend and I waited at the entrance gate for hours and finally got to meet the lead singer when he stumbled outside after his set. I wore the paper admission wristband for a week as a souvenir. My mother fixated on the wristband in those few days—it looked ugly, she said, and more important, though she didn't say this aloud, it was a symbol of my rebellion. My parents listened to classic soul, South African vocalists; hip-hop was tolerated. Rock music was foreign, devilish. A week after the concert, my father drove us to a store and we waited in the car while he went inside. My mother and I, left behind, started to argue. I was in the back seat, she was in the passenger's-side seat, and as our fight reached its crescendo, she leapt on me from the front seat, tearing the band from my wrist. "I hate this thing!" she screamed, then chucked it out the window.

I grew to understand that she hid her past from me out of fear. She knew that the truth of her younger days would only inspire my rebellion even more. Her antagonism toward me was likely rooted in the same fear: the fear of having a black girl in a world that despised them. Or perhaps I'm too easy on her. I was adventurous, unreservedly ambitious, nonconformist. I was just like her when she was young.

In 2010, at twenty-six, I entered graduate school at Columbia University in New York City, not far from where I had spent three years working for a publishing house while concealing my desire to write the same kind of books that we produced. My

MFA program was industry-focused, competitive, and almost entirely white.

In each year, there were a handful of black people, mostly women, and I quickly made friends with one who was near graduation at the time I started. She was a great writer—daring, ambitious, and militant to boot. One evening in a bar in Greenwich Village, a white woman around our age sat at our table. The white woman marveled at her dreadlocks. "Do you like Bob Marley?" the white woman asked vapidly. "Do you like anal sex?" my friend countered, not missing a beat.

She told me that relationships between male professors and female students were common in my program, that some of these relationships ended up benefiting the woman's career. The transaction was obvious but unsaid. She told me which professors to look out for. And she told me, in no uncertain terms, not to participate. "They'll never respect you," she said with gravity, and I knew I never would.

Over time, I saw the relationships between professors and students materialize from the sidelines. They never interested me. I have always had a natural instinct to recognize exploitation and am repulsed by it in relationships; in this way, I consider myself very lucky. My mother often bragged about her ex-boyfriends and maintained friendships with many of them her whole life. "Men are so easy to manipulate," she once scoffed to me. She taught me to demand respect in relationships and not to settle for anything less.

There was another factor that never let me engage in such scenarios: my ambition. I wanted desperately to prove how talented

I was and earn my achievements on merit. I knew I was good enough to compete with anyone on an even playing field. During those years in grad school, I began to recognize that these relationships composed a shadow economy of their own, where the work was sex and the currency was our bodies. I respected sex work, but I wanted to be a writer.

In my second year of grad school, I took a course with a notorious professor who was also the editor of one of the most prestigious literary magazines in the world. His relationships with Columbia students were an open secret. He kept these women in his coterie, kept their company at industry parties, employed them at the magazine, and sometimes published them. A story in his pages meant an almost instant ticket to success. He had published the black woman writer, though nothing had happened between them, and they had a friendly rapport. At the same time that she warned me about him, she encouraged me to take his class for what it could do for my career. I took her advice, determined to make a professional connection, knowing I had to handle the situation carefully. Naively, I tried my best to ignore the rumors I'd heard and prove myself as a writer, on my own terms.

Our first class was delayed because, the school informed us, he had recently undergone surgery. He showed up to school on the first day in a matching sweatsuit. He was a modest-looking man: tall and skinny, with translucent skin and blooms of rosacea around his nose and cheeks. He stood proudly in front of the class with his chest puffed out, even in his pitiful sweatsuit. It was clear that he got off on the adulation of the students in the classroom, of their attention to his every word, of their fear. I noticed this and was determined, from day one, never to feed his ego.

My circumspection only seemed to titillate him further and he took a liking to me almost instantly. He called on me frequently and seemed delighted as I responded to his sometimes enigmatic questions with confidence. I challenged him openly, as I did everyone, and he seemed excited that I was so clearly unintimidated by him.

His fascination with me did not go unnoticed by the rest of the class. The chairs and tables were arranged in a large circle in the center of the room. I usually arrived late to class and sat in one of the chairs that lined the back wall. One day, a few weeks into the semester, he stopped speaking mid-lecture and beckoned me forward. "Why don't you sit here, Zinzi," he cooed, patting the seat beside him.

"No, thanks," I murmured from the back of the room.

After that day, my classmates began to tease me about the professor. One day, I ran into a classmate in the hallway. "He has a crush on you," he snickered, smiling wryly. I had dated this student briefly and still had lingering feelings for him. I felt my face flush with embarrassment.

On the last day of class we met at a nearby bar that served as the program's unofficial hangout. Knowing that the professor might act inappropriately in that environment, I showed up an hour late, just as everyone was ordering their last round. The professor was buzzed and giddy. Before I left, he leaned toward me. "You have an ear for language," he breathed, "send me a story."

Though I was uneasy with his behavior, I felt elated. I had played the situation just right, I thought, having proven my talent while steadily ducking his advances. I slid out of the bar shortly thereafter, excited that my big break might be just around the corner.

After classes ended, I labored over a short story for months. When I had finally finished it, I emailed it to him. Months went by and then almost a year with no response. Even though my chances were dimmed, I still held out hope. Maybe he'd been busy or incapacitated. Maybe he'd lost my email.

In the interim, I signed up with an agent recommended by one of my other professors. Not long after, she followed up with him. The rejection came shortly after. I was used to them by then; I'd started submitting my work a couple of years ago and had had a couple of stories published in smaller journals. My agent forwarded me his reply. I remember opening the email and my heart dropping into my stomach. It was curt and dismissive. I didn't know if his response was based on my writing, which I could accept, or our interactions. Thinking about it made me feel dirty, and I resented that it might have factored into the equation at all.

I heard about the workshop for writers of color in my first year of graduate school. It was held in Berkeley, California, and was founded by one of the most famous contemporary writers, whom

I deeply admired. I idolized The Author's career and the political, often confrontational nature of his writing. At the workshop, his teaching philosophy was built around empowering multicultural writers. I found the approach inspiring. I was eager to soak in this environment and perhaps speak to The Author himself. I knew I had so much to learn from him.

The black woman writer spoke about the workshop in rhapsodic terms. For her, literary success followed a strict, predetermined path: meet the right people, publish a book before age thirty, teach at the right schools. Success in our field was so unpredictable; her confidence in this manner was comforting. According to her, the workshop was one stop along the way. I applied as soon as I was eligible and received a partial scholarship. The rest I paid for with my meager savings and student loans. I was intent on going, no matter the cost.

My week in Berkeley was dreamlike. I'd visited Northern California only once when I was younger and my love for the place still held. It was an unreal place, with azure skies larger than any I'd seen in the East, friendly people, and the feeling of newness. I met writers who looked like me, with the same political concerns and urgency about our work. No longer sidelined in our mostly white grad-school classes, we took center stage at the workshop. It was restorative, invigorating, and—it would turn out for me—life-changing.

On the first day, we gathered in a meeting room, more than one hundred of us all together. We played a game to introduce ourselves one by one: We supplied our basic biographical information and then, in true Berkeley form, announced to the group what our ancestors were telling us that day. I was one of the last to speak, and the whole time I watched the others give their answers, I grew more and more nervous. I'd never been asked such a question, and my East Coast cynicism didn't allow me to play along. I decided to simply be honest. "I've never spoken to my ancestors before," I said flatly, expecting awkward silence. Instead, the entire room burst into laughter. My answer, it seemed, won me some friends, and we walked together out of the building. On the curb just outside sat The Author. As I walked by, he looked up at me. "Hey," he offered casually, "I really like what you said." He smiled. I walked on air the rest of the day.

The shortcomings of mainstream feminism (what many call "white feminism") are more widely understood now—how it sidelines and diminishes those of minoritized racial, gender, and other identities, reproducing many of the same inequities as sexist culture. Kimberlé Crenshaw's theory of intersectionality addressed this interlocking system of oppression. If you're a black woman, you may have felt this personally. That was my story, too.

I detest the contemporary obsession with calling oneself a feminist. This matters much less than how you behave. But one's political evolution seems like an important story to tell, if it can help others.

I don't agree that literature should be utilitarian. I believe in art for art's sake, and in the internal conflict that our encounters with its highest forms engender. However, I believe that art should indeed have purpose.

For most of my life, I did not want to admit that men held power over me. I didn't think I needed that word—*feminism*—even if I needed other women. But when I needed it, it was there for me.

In my second year of graduate school, inspired by the workshop at Berkeley, I put together an event with The Author. In it, he would speak about his approach to writing, informed by considerations of race and difference, that I'd admired for so long. I worked hard on making the event happen.

I was very busy at the time: In addition to the obligations of my coursework, I also held a fellowship that required me to work thirty hours a week in the graduate office. I was involved in several extracurriculars, sent my work out for publication, and interned at a national magazine once a week. The production and planning of an event of professional quality was not something I had time for, but I undertook it because The Author and his work meant so much to me.

The event took months to plan. There was the scheduling, the logistics of The Author's arrival, the selection of the audience. I convinced a financially conservative department to buy a book and lunch for each attendee. I carefully composed, then workshopped, several questions to ask The Author during the program, which I sent to him beforehand so that he would be prepared. I choreographed the program down to each moment.

On the day of the event, I arrived early and assembled the room. I welcomed the guests excitedly. I was nervous but eager to get started. I knew the day would be important, possibly one of the most important of my career thus far.

As I stood at the front of the classroom watching the guests take their seats, I checked my watch. It was almost time to meet him outside, as we'd agreed beforehand. As I started toward the door, I noticed him at the back of the classroom. He looked around in disbelief. He found my eyes and mouthed, "What the fuck is this?" I was crushed. What had I done wrong?

I walked to the back of the room and shook his hand, then led him to the front. I introduced him to the audience and showed him to a chair I'd arranged next to mine, facing the classroom. He ignored it. Instead, he stood and immediately began speaking. Knowing the event would no longer go as planned, I took a chair in the front row of desks.

Pacing back and forth, he launched into a prepared monologue. Occasionally, I tried shakily to interject one of my prepared questions. He generally ignored or mocked me. Describing an element of plot, he asked if I knew the name for a certain technique. When I admitted I didn't, he scoffed, "They didn't teach you that at Columbia?" The class erupted in laughter. My face turned hot. I wished to disappear into my chair.

Since that day, I have spoken in front of crowds of hundreds. I've done events all over the world, appeared on television and live radio, and dealt with hecklers of all stripes along the way. Never have I felt as uncomfortable in front of an audience as I did that day surrounded by my peers. The more uncomfortable I became, the more animated it seemed to make him. I felt stupid, embarrassed, and humiliated. I can still feel the tension in each part of my body, how I prayed, at every moment, every time his eye caught mine, that it would end. Looking back, I realize that humiliation was an essential part of his performance. Someone had to be the prop, the straight man, and for whatever reason, he chose me. In the moment, I understood only that I was less than him and deserving of this treatment.

Finally, when it was over, I accompanied him out of the room and into the stairwell opposite to escort him out of the building. I thanked him heartily for coming, masking my discomfort with cheeriness. The door to the stairwell closed.

I followed him down the stairs and when he reached the landing he paused. We stood across from each other. His anger melted away and turned to affection. I had felt this before. Time slowed as he leaned toward me. I felt a familiar mix of fear and flattery. He called me beautiful. He moved in toward my lips and at the last moment, as our lips were about to touch, he planted a kiss on my cheek. He said something else, smiling. I stood there frozen, trying to parse what had just happened. Before I knew it, he was gone.

I had some context for this behavior. I'd found myself in similar situations with writers before, but none so overt. The black woman writer's words echoed in my head. I knew what he wanted, and I felt disgusted by it. This part of our interaction was clear, and even though it made me uncomfortable, I felt relief that maybe he didn't hate me after all.

Later, I found a short, affectionate email from The Author

thanking me for the event in my inbox. It was unusual—generally it was the host who sent a thank-you. I connected it to the behavior in the stairwell and I ignored it, uninterested in reciprocating. Instead, I sent a predrafted thank you that I'd had approved by my supervisor in the graduate office days before. In it, I included a request to write a blog post about the event for the magazine I interned at, which I'd also run by my boss days ago. I thought it would be good publicity for The Author and a chance for me to write about something I was passionate about: a win-win. My editor agreed. I thought it was a simple request.

The Author replied immediately in his short, casual tone, the response lacking punctuation and riddled with typos. He was angry. He was offended by the blog post idea and accused me of trying to steal his intellectual property. He told me that he had been wary of agreeing to the event and that his friends had warned him against it. My request had proven his suspicions correct.

In a panic, I showed the email to my supervisor at Columbia. I drafted an apology email as quickly and as carefully as I could. I showed it to my officemates and friends and asked for their feedback, terrified of further upsetting him. I hit send. To my relief, I heard nothing from him again.

The day after, I told the man I was dating about the kiss and showed him the affectionate email. He was shocked. He chuckled at The Author's latest email. Another friend called him an egomaniac.

In the years afterward, I would repeat the story of the kiss to friends and acquaintances, but I was too ashamed to tell them the rest: my humiliation in the classroom, his email brimming with anger and accusation. I so admired The Author that I believed him more than I did myself. I was stupid and out of line for asking to write about the event. I continued to admire his work, to teach it to students, and to recommend his workshop in Berkeley. To continue my admiration for him I had to further discredit myself. I tried hard to forget the ugliness and deep unease he engendered in me that day. I was wrong and he was right.

Until my book was published, the event was one of the proudest achievements of my career. Every time I updated my résumé and sent it to employers, every time I described it in an interview or a meeting, I heard the author's mocking voice, his disapproving looks, the laughter of the audience. Most of all, I remembered the time in the stairwell, then his rage at me in his email. I remembered the rejection from the notorious professor. It all seemed to confirm that there was something deeply wrong with me. I wasn't the words I'd written or the lines on my résumé, but the butt of his jokes and the pitiful, small reflection in his eyes.

In June of 2012, a couple of months after The Author's visit, I finished my graduate coursework, the culmination of two years of grueling work in and outside the classroom. I'd found a job at the Columbia Publishing Course, a program that funneled young Ivy League graduates into careers like the one I'd left to become a grad student. In more ways than one, I felt that I'd regressed, that I'd failed.

On the first day, when I was on my lunch break, I received a phone call from my normally stoic father. He was in tears. He'd just gotten back from my mother's doctor visit. It was pouring rain that day, and I'd stepped into the vestibule of the building, shaking off my umbrella, when I heard him choke out, "The doctor says . . . she has weeks to live," between sobs. She had been diagnosed with multiple myeloma two years prior, had been undergoing regular treatments that, to our knowledge, kept the cancer in check. That day, we found out that it had bloomed all over her body, tumors bending her neck at a severe angle, weakening her beyond repair. In shock, I quit my job immediately and made my way home to Philadelphia, where I would stay for the next six months until she died.

During that time, I let go of the anger that had built up toward her during my childhood. I needed to, in order to move on. How could I be angry for her simply trying to survive, to protect her family? This is what I told myself. Without that anger to protect me, her critical voice often echoed in my head; louder even, at times, than when she was alive.

The other story I must tell you is this: In 2013, about one year after my mother died and slightly more after the event with The Author, I was sexually assaulted and almost raped on a trip to South Africa. The confluence of these events, in hindsight, devastates, but is also awfully common. Victims of sexual violence are often chosen because of their vulnerability, and—though I failed to recognize it myself at the time—I was distressingly vulnerable.

I told no one aside from my then-boyfriend about the assault and barely admitted it to myself, hoping to will away what had happened with silence. In the days subsequent, the statistic that one out of every six women in America has been sexually assaulted often came to mind; that more than 40 percent of women are assaulted in South Africa. I told myself that I was privileged, and I wasn't physically harmed. I wasn't actually raped. I told myself to feel lucky. I wanted to feel selfless more than I wanted to feel scared.

And I was relieved to realize that I didn't have to wear those titles—victim, survivor—if I didn't want to. They didn't fit the person I thought I was, the person I was so intent on making myself. But to do so meant that I didn't admit what happened at all. I kept it quiet, and that act of silence constituted a lie that I told myself over and over: Nothing happened to you, you are fine. I hate lying, I've never done it well, and in the following years, my body began to reject that lie.

As The Author moved toward me in the stairwell I knew, because of how practiced it felt, that he had done this to other women. I knew it deep in my body, even though, at that point, I had no point of reference for that kind of behavior. The body is a magnificent machine, full of ancient signals and independent functions that initiate millions of processes to inform and protect itself. My body told me all I needed to know, but it had no idea of how many other women there might be.

. . .

Though I never complained, those months I spent in Philadelphia as my mother's caretaker were harrowing. She became my full-time charge; I was with her all the time. I gave her her medicine and tracked it on a two-page spreadsheet my father had drafted. I made her soft, bland meals of scrambled eggs and applesauce. I cleaned her mouth after she ate. I helped her to the bathroom. I cleaned her up when she couldn't make it to the toilet in time. I helped her wash herself. I helped her walk to the car, then wheeled her into her doctor's appointments, took notes as the doctor spoke, then wheeled her home and put her to bed. I watched her cry so many times and somehow found a way to tell her that things weren't so bad. That I was okay and she would be fine. I don't know what was worse, watching the excruciation her body went through or witnessing her shrivel from the proud, independent woman she once was.

I was twenty-six. The experience scarred me irrevocably. Looking back on all the damage it caused, I sometimes think I made a mistake. I could have left the work to someone else, even though it would have been difficult for my parents to afford, kept only the memories of her as I knew her most of her life: a strong, in-control woman. But along with the pain of those days was a love so thick it covered us every day. I don't think I can regret a single moment.

I developed chronic insomnia during that time. I never had a good night's sleep for all the months I cared for her. Just as I was about to drift off, I would be seized by the thought of her dying.

I would jolt awake every few hours, always at the ready. Sleep felt like lowering my head below water, like I was losing what little control I still had.

Long after those days had gone, those sleepless nights persisted. I would sleep a couple of hours after watching the sun rise, then sleep the whole next day. The entire time, I buzzed with nervous energy, halfway between the land of the dead and that of the living. My mind was always fuzzy; I missed meetings and appointments, outings with friends. Every day I tried to grab hold of some normalcy, tried to pretend I wasn't still reeling from the trauma. But one can only pretend for so long.

In 2014, shortly after meeting my husband, The Author released an essay about the experience of writers of color in graduate creative writing programs. The essay echoed many of the tortured feelings that I experienced while in my program and that I had tried to address through student organizations and initiatives, like the very event I'd created for him. Many other writers also identified with this message and the essay received considerable attention, including at the artist colony where my husband and I spent our first months together.

Everyone, including me, was impressed by the essay. The other writers and I praised it, but my husband sulked. He dismissed the essay as hollow and The Author's work as overrated and lacking in substance. I interpreted his criticisms as an indictment of my values of multiculturalism and inclusion. My husband insisted that his appraisal was based on his technical assessment of The

Author's work and that The Author's shortcomings as a writer were often overlooked in favor of his message. I defended The Author and his writing as my own. In my mind, the two were inextricably bound. I'd still never told anyone the whole story of what he had done. I believed I was wrong and The Author was right, and unquestioned, that narrative grew to encompass everything.

Thus began one of our first arguments. It continued for some time with me defending The Author and him critiquing his work. Slowly, my position weakened. I had to admit that there were limits to his artistry and lacunae in his worldview. At some point, I told my husband about the kiss. He erupted in anger. It confirmed everything he thought about The Author. "You don't understand," I countered. I attempted to hold fast to my admiration for The Author, for the first time feeling my reverence for him, and my whole world, slip.

And then a few years later, in the fall of 2017 (shortly after my novel was published), the secrets that so many of us had held close began to be disclosed and, with it, anger pent up over many years flowed. Events coalesced into what would be looked at, in retrospect, as the beginning of a movement.

By this time, the black woman writer and I were no longer in touch, but her warning came back to mind. The men whose deeds were in whispers were named in the open. Every week, it seemed, an idol fell, men who were formerly considered untouchable. An article was published about the notorious professor; he had resigned from his job at the literary magazine and decamped to the UK. Everywhere, power crumbled.

The moment comported with me in a deep way, with my fundamental suspicion of power and faith in justice. Like so many others, this time led me to reassess my past experiences. I found fault in myself for times when I stayed silent. I gained more admiration for those who had the courage to speak up.

I saw The Author's name mentioned online in conjunction with a variety of misbehaviors, and I thought back on our interactions. By this time, I was an author and a teacher myself with a firm understanding of right and wrong. I could no longer blame myself for what he did to me. I granted myself innocence and grace, which I'd denied for so long in order to continue to hold him in high regard. From this new perspective, his behavior looked worse and worse.

I didn't intend to be part of that movement. Most of the women coming forward in my industry were white, and I always felt unsure about my place among them. But I felt moral clarity, and for the first time, finding myself with a public voice, I felt compelled to speak.

In the comments of one of my Facebook posts, I wrote vaguely about my encounter with The Author. I didn't use his name—I was afraid to—but what I did say was enough for others to know who I was speaking of, and they replied with their own experiences. They were also angry, tired, frustrated. It was also enough for a reporter to contact me by email. She had been looking into a number of tips related to The Author. She said that my account sounded similar to others she'd heard and she wanted to chat further.

Soon, I received a message from an unfamiliar account. In the small thumbnail, I could see a fair-skinned woman with brown hair looking softly into the camera, her hand cradling her cheek. Her words were caring but deliberate, and she concluded each message with a heart emoji. She was a writer of sci-fi novels. We also both happened to be from Pennsylvania. I found her plain-spoken, confident, humble. She told me about a professional encounter years ago with The Author. He had publicly humiliated her at a professional dinner and yelled the word *rape* several times in her face. She had left the scenario deeply disturbed, and with the feeling that he had mistreated many other people as well.

In the story of this entire episode, of my lost years, this moment would be the beginning; when Alice saw a cuddly rabbit and decided to follow him. This is the unassuming start, after which things would spiral unbelievably out of control.

But I didn't know this at the time. I typed my reply to the sci-fi writer and pushed send.

A few months later, in 2018, I traveled from Los Angeles to New York for an awards ceremony. Since grad school, in part due to The Author, I'd studiously avoided literary events. But this was the biggest event so far of my career, and I was supposed to share the stage with at least one other writer I admired.

I indulged in the free hotel room, I packed a nice dress and a beautiful beaded collar that I'd bought in Nigeria. I hadn't had an occasion to wear it until then.

My plane to New York City was delayed and I arrived at JFK airport at 3 a.m. The flight was bumpy and my insomnia meant I couldn't sleep on planes even in the most placid of conditions. It was an unnerving, white-knuckle ride. Once I landed, inside the taxi en route to my hotel in Manhattan, I opened Facebook on my phone. Almost immediately, I saw a link shared to my timeline: an essay written by The Author.

The thumbnail contained a photo of a young boy looking just beyond the camera. I swallowed, then flipped past it. I kept scrolling and noticed it shared many more times by my friends and acquaintances, each time accompanied by a caption with fawning praise. A few of these were written by friends to whom I'd told my story, who had their own stories about The Author. Finally, I clicked through to the essay. By this time, I'd started to be more honest about how uncomfortable he'd made me. I read the first few sentences and felt like I was following him to that dark stairwell once again, feeling the door close. I stopped.

I saw the young boy up close: The Author in child form. The child in no way resembled the man: He was young, innocent, and something else. His eyes were tired, the look of pain behind them. I felt empathy for the child, who The Author now, at long last, declared a victim. But something inside me, heightened by fatigue, wouldn't let me finish reading the essay. My sympathy for the boy sat uncomfortably next to my knowledge of the man he'd become. I knew that abusive behavior, both violent and nonviolent, is often learned in childhood, and this fact requires compassion for those who do harm. To me it seemed that The Author's gambit was immediately clear: to compete with the women he'd wronged for victimhood.

The truth was that there was symmetry to our stories. Though I couldn't admit it at the time, I was keeping the secret of my own sexual assault in South Africa, from others and from myself.

I knew this to be true of any women The Author may have mistreated, because it is the story of women throughout history. It does not excuse the replication of that abuse upon others.

I felt anger. I closed Facebook, the image of the boy still there in my mind.

At the awards ceremony, The Author's name was on everyone's lips. Many people had read the essay and questioned his intentions in publishing it. Some writers I held in high esteem had voiced similar feelings on Twitter that day. Just like me, they speculated that he had released the article in order to preempt revelations about his behavior, which they conjectured would likely be exposed soon. Some at the awards ceremony knew about my experience with him. They encouraged me to speak out about it. I talked with another writer who had an experience with The Author very similar to mine. Unlike me, she was resolved to never say anything about it. Knowing there was someone else made me realize I had to do something. Facing her, my sense of urgency rose, along with the realization that if I said nothing, no one else would.

. . .

A few weeks later, as I was getting ready to attend the Sydney Writers' Festival, I noticed that The Author was headlining the festival. His name was on the festival's Twitter feed and all over their promotional emails. Every time I saw it I felt like I had been thrown down a dark tunnel. As the date approached and their promotion of him increased, I began to feel more and more nervous. I thought, in horror, of what would happen if we were together in the greenroom. I was scared that he would remember me and still be angry, recalling the tone of his final email to me. Would he tell the other authors that I was that bratty MFA kid who threatened to steal his work? Even worse, would he not remember me and try to corner me again? Would he be more aggressive this time, now that we were on an equal footing and outside an educational setting, with booze flowing liberally, as it always does at literary events? These questions circled my mind daily.

Since we moved to California, I had been using cannabis to sleep. I'd take a pill or a bite of brownie an hour before bed and feel myself melt into incomprehension. It worked for a long time, and I felt my physical and mental health improve with increased sleep.

But in the weeks before Sydney, flooded with anxiety about encountering The Author, anytime that I wasn't at work, I was getting stoned. My tolerance built up so that I was taking incredibly high amounts—sometimes hundreds of milligrams at a time—just to feel its effects. I didn't answer the phone, didn't reply to emails.

One evening, when we were entertaining a friend for dinner, I'd gotten stoned all day, then had a glass of wine after she arrived. We sat chatting on the couch while my husband prepared dinner in the kitchen. She was a poet and we discussed her current projects. A few minutes into the conversation, everything went black. When I came to, the friend and my husband were looking over me, worried. I had lost consciousness midsentence. My husband carried me to our bedroom, where I slept while they continued the evening without me. The poet friend reached out afterward asking if I was all right. I brushed off the incident, saying I hadn't been feeling well, which was basically true.

My husband and I were making love in the bedroom of our new house. The lights were off, and I was high enough to forget my troubles but also where I was, and suddenly, I was somewhere else. He became someone unfamiliar, and then I was beside him, trembling and crying. He broke down also, scared and worried. It took some time to comfort me.

What is fear but feeling lost someplace other than where you want to be?

My terror built until finally I decided to do something about it. I searched the festival website and read the profiles of their event staff. I found a young assistant who had worked for a women's charity. I wrote to her:

> I have been nervous about being at the festival at the same time as The Author because of a past interaction, and I would like to ask that we not be near each other at any point. . . .

Sydney is not very far from the West Coast of the United States—a fifteen-hour flight, about the same time from New York to Johannesburg, a flight I'd taken every couple of years since I was six months old. I'd never been farther west than California—nor farther east than the Persian Gulf—and in the spring of 2018 I felt an eerie sense of peace flying through the far reaches of the Pacific Ocean, like I was hurtling off into some middle earth, so far away from America and everything I knew. When I arrived in Sydney, I was pleased to realize that part of Australia resembled South Africa in its climate, its foliage, its brick houses with terra-cotta roofs—no wonder so many South Africans emigrate there. Part of me felt at home immediately upon arrival.

My hotel room had a freestanding tub that sat next to a comfy king bed. This was where I spent most of my first few days, soaking in the bathtub, popping cannabis pills I'd smuggled in my luggage, and pondering what I would do if I encountered The Author.

I'd been trading emails with the sci-fi author, had learned of more stories posted on social media about The Author. I'd also kept in touch with the reporter who emailed me. I'd told her everything that happened, everything I knew, and she told me she couldn't write the story until someone else was willing to come forward publicly. So far, that was a tall order. The women that we knew of were minorities at early stages in their careers. They feared, rightfully, the type of retaliation The Author could marshal against them. From the behavior I'd witnessed, I knew he was aggressive and impulsive, propelled by a huge ego. At the same time, I sensed that his back was on the ropes. Though they didn't name him, many writers were speculating on social media about him.

An idea had started to take shape in my mind in the days before my journey. With the high-profile nature of the festival, I knew that if I brought these issues to light, they would soon go public. I knew that this was one of the few chances, if not the only one, to expose The Author's behavior. My fear began to morph into resolve. I realized that I could stay in my room hiding or I could take matters into my own hands. I asked my husband and my most rebellious friend for their advice. They told me to go ahead.

The next morning, I went to the hotel restaurant for breakfast. I found many young women writers who I both knew and had a connection to, and I lingered over breakfast, writing and occasionally striking up a conversation. A couple of hours in, a writer whom I'd met in Los Angeles walked in wheeling her suitcase, fresh off a plane. We traded pleasantries and asked about each other's events. I'd noticed that she was slated to appear on a panel with The Author. She was a young, beautiful woman who would surely be in his crosshairs. When I told her the outlines of my experience and warned her to be careful, she told me I was the third person to do so. I told her about the last few months, the stories from other women, the reporter.

"I'm thinking I should say something about it," I offered meekly.

"You definitely should," she said.

The day of The Author's panel, I borrowed a bike from my hotel. I set off in the morning and rode north through downtown Sydney. I rode for hours through Hyde Park and past the Royal Botanical Garden. My mind was clear. I reached the opera house and pedaled right up to the front steps. I sat at an open-air café and snapped pictures of the water, ate my lunch of fish and chips while surrounded by seagulls waiting to steal it from my plate. I felt that I was nearing a point of no return, the day mired in finality.

The panel was in the auditorium of a university, housing a crowd of around two hundred. On stage, The Author sat next to my friend, and all through the event he stared at her, and when he spoke, his voice trilled and his eyes lit in her direction.

I'd thought through what I would do in advance. I knew what I would say and in what order, when I would leave in order to avoid questioning or confrontation.

When the panel moderator called for questions, I approached the volunteer who was passing the mic around the crowd. I took it. I asked The Author if he'd like to apologize for how he'd treated me so many years ago. The crowd gasped as I headed for the exit. When I was almost at the door, The Author asked if he could respond. I turned back around to face him. The Author looked calmly in my direction. He said that when he wrote the essay he had been at a true low point in his life, contemplating suicide, and a friend had told him that he needed to make a change. He then paused, allowing the crowd to applaud him.

As I turned toward the door again, I yelled into the auditorium that I knew this friend and I'd learned that he had been accused of sexual misconduct. The crowd booed. I burst through the doors in tears.

At almost the same moment, a white woman around my age came streaming into the lobby, also crying. We hugged each other.

"I just couldn't sit there any longer," she said, "I had to see if you were okay."

We walked together out of the building, where I found my bike locked in front.

"Do you want to go somewhere?" she asked me.

She walked beside me while I wheeled my borrowed bicycle all the way back to the hotel. There, we grabbed seats at the bar and she told me that she worked for a Sydney publishing house. I recognized something in her that was like me. This was her first time at the festival. We traded publishing stories; she told me which projects she was excited about. We laughed together. Her small gesture of friendship in that moment gave me everything I needed.

When I got back to my room, I realized that what I said might never be covered outside of that auditorium, or that if it was it would be in a way that was biased toward The Author. Most of the audience seemed to support him, after all. So I made a post on Twitter saying that The Author had kissed me against my will back in graduate school. It took off immediately. Press appeared at my event the next morning asking me questions about my tweet, and my story was the subject of headlines from every major international outlet.

I got word that The Author had left the conference early. He released a statement through *The New York Times*: "I take responsibility for my past," it read. "That is the reason I made the decision to tell the truth of my rape and its damaging aftermath. . . . We must continue to teach all men about consent and boundaries."

I again felt like I was floating outside of my body, watching someone else in my place. Unlike the time when my husband and I made love, this time I felt like I was watching myself in a movie, buffeted by the festival's handlers, greeted by cheering crowds and reporters shouting questions at me from the press line. I was unable to compute the reality of what was happening to me. And even now, when I think about what had happened, it seems impossibly remote, fuzzy, as if my mind had covered those memories in cotton.

My last event at the festival was a panel with other women authors in a huge auditorium with hundreds of people in attendance. Before we went onstage, I struck up a conversation with another writer. She told me that she had friends who were named, under pseudonyms, as lovers in The Author's essay whom he'd mistreated. She looked at me, taking in my face, my hair. "They look just like you," she told me.

. . .

After Sydney, I returned to South Africa for the first time since my assault in 2013. My flight had a layover in Abu Dhabi, and by the time I arrived at my hotel room in Johannesburg I was delirious from lack of sleep. My cousin Kim met me in my hotel room. Whenever I returned to Johannesburg, on my first day back, my cousins always gave me an update: who's married, who's not speaking to whom, who's died. Kim, lounging on the bed in my hotel room, imparted the news that Faryn Fine, who was our cousin's best friend since high school, was dead. She'd smothered her toddler son with a pillow, and a few days later, she was found in her friend's garage.

I met Faryn when I was in high school. Her name echoed her beautiful, delicate features: almond eyes that looked down an aquiline nose and soft pink lips. She was so striking that she seemed cut from a magazine—but tough. In most pictures she wore baggy cargo pants and a slim-fitting tank top. Usually she was slouched in the driver's seat of a car, her long legs curled beneath the steering wheel. Her eyes were usually bloodshot, one eyebrow cocked cheekily, her lips in a scowl.

I had thought of her occasionally before this trip. The father of Faryn's child was abusive. Sadistic, Kim told me. He tortured her for many years, and when they broke up, he threatened to take her child away. Faryn felt she had no other choice, so she killed her son. Held a pillow over his face until he stopped moving. She went to jail, got out, and a few days later, her friends found her hanging in their garage.

I sat there a moment, reeling. My mind made a quick calculation: How much despair pushes you to take such action? I couldn't compute it.

The last leg of my South African tour was a book festival in a sleepy town in the Western Cape's wine country. I met women who inspired me, and we stayed up late trading stories over dinner. One told me about her ex-boyfriend who abused her, and, with tears in her eyes, how her friends abandoned her when she admitted it to them.

The greenroom for the festival was located in a small, elegant cottage with a green backyard outfitted with patio furniture. On my last day, I sat among a group of women and noticed an editor crying on a bench at the edge of the yard. A stream of authors took turns comforting her. We soon learned that her niece, who'd been taking care of her young child, had passed away unexpectedly. The child was alone a few hours away with the dead body. There was no one there to help.

Over the next couple of hours, a ride was arranged for her, a plan took shape out of panicked indeterminacy. But the air of tragedy lingered, and the complimentary wine loosened our lips. The women began sharing stories. A black author told us a series of stories that progressed in brutality, her eyes glossy with tears. Finally, she told us about her sister. Her husband beat her for a long time and killed her by pushing her out of a window. We could do little more than mutter "shame" in response.

My feet never quite touched the ground in South Africa. I

didn't sleep well. I drank too much. I needed to forget what had happened, to me and to the other women I spoke to. They could see my wounds gaping open, an invitation. I was hollow and their pain fit right inside.

The sci-fi writer and I kept in touch, along with two other writers who made public statements alleging mistreatment by The Author. One of them wrote about being berated by him at a public reading in grad school. The other recounted meeting him at a restaurant after he contacted her on a dating site. He made racialized comments about her appearance and when she got upset, he pulled her into his lap and wrapped his arms around her. She cried until he escorted her out of the restaurant.

We put out a public call on Twitter for anyone who'd had similar experiences with The Author. In response, we received dozens of accounts from colleagues, friends, and strangers alleging a range of behaviors. Many of the accounts centered on the Berkeley workshop.

A group of alumni of the Berkeley workshop published an open letter that read in part: "Many of us have been aware of sexual and other forms of abuse at the workshop stemming back over a decade. This behavior was an 'open secret' . . . and we have received many testimonies from fellows who attempted to bring it to the attention of [the workshop]."

We received several messages from people who others would later warn us were friends of The Author fishing for information. "He likes to control his image," one of them wrote.

Several people unconnected to us wrote stories of their own about The Author. Some tweeted about him belittling them at public events and in classrooms. Some of them wrote about their relationships with him.

One woman wrote about an evening she spent with him after a reading. She was a scholar in residence at a nearby college. "As the night progressed," she wrote, "I noticed that his behavior became more and more hostile, especially after I told him to 'slow down,' for he was moving too fast with his sexual advances . . . it resulted in his turning deliberately mean." He made a racialized remark about her hair; she excused herself from the event and cried on the way home.

A woman who was named in his essay wrote about their relationship, which began while she was a student of his. The essay is lyrical and moving, and she writes of herself in the third person: "Each night together, he would swear her to silence in the early hours of the morning. Somehow that silence continued. After spending the night in her bed, he would insist, 'This is nothing, you know that, right?' which she quickly translated to mean, 'I am nothing.'"

Another writer, who had a sexual relationship with The Author, wrote an essay critical of his work. He promised to ruin her. "And maybe he did," she wrote.

> Things were hard. Harder than they should have been. People posted about how "crazy" I was. Truly vile and abusive shit. I had become a writer in part because I am an introvert. I never wanted the attention to be on me as a person, only on my writing. But there I was, being

> dragged through the mud. . . . I could never get a call back from the *New Yorker*, or the *NY Times*, when I pitched poems or stories or op-eds. Maybe it was [The Author]. Or maybe it was something else. My vagina. My book covers. My lack of an MFA. My honesty. . . .

I saw parts of my own experience, and parts of myself, in each of these stories.

Looking back on this experience from years on, what stings the most is the knowledge that, to many, I am nothing outside of my involvement with The Author. That all I have worked for and all that I am—good, bad, and in between—has been reduced to a footnote in The Author's story. If I have one regret, it is that.

In the end, I spoke off the record with five reporters who were investigating the story, hoping that articles would be published and the truth made public. I never published the full account of my encounter with The Author on Twitter or anywhere else, knowing that unless it was published by trusted, professional reporters, it might be mishandled and distorted. To this day, no articles have been published with the stories of his accusers.

We shared the information we received by email with reporters. While this happened, I saw investigations published about other public figures accused of the same behavior as The Author, validating the accusers' accounts. The accused faced accountability. I waited for our turn and grew resentful and bitter when it never came.

In May 2018, I received an email from the Title IX office at Columbia University, which informed me that it had received a report that I had been subjected to sexual harassment by one of its affiliates, in violation of their *Employee Policy and Procedures on Discrimination, Harassment, Sexual Assault, Domestic Violence, Dating Violence, and Stalking.* The policy, which they attached to the email, defined sexual harassment as:

> Unwelcome sexual advances, requests for sexual favors, requests for sexual contact, and other verbal, physical, or visual conduct of a sexual nature constitutes sexual harassment when: [. . .] such unwelcome conduct is intentional, serves no legitimate purpose, and involves contact with parts of another individual's body which may cause that person to feel degraded or abused; or when the behavior is for the purpose of gratifying the actor's sexual desire . . .

I spoke with representatives from their office on the phone and they asked me to file a report about my encounter with The Author. I had followed the story of Emma Sulkowicz, the Columbia undergraduate who'd carried her dorm room mattress, on which she alleged that she'd been raped, with her for eight months. After a Title IX hearing, Columbia found the man not responsible and he was able to graduate. I was afraid of The

Author's anger and power. I told the office I wasn't ready to file a report, but to keep the file open in case I did in the future. But I never did, and eventually I learned that the statute of limitations on the case had expired.

The three other women and I were contacted by the university that employed him and we supplied our testimonies as well as the leads we'd received. When the literary journal for which he served as editor refused to fire him, their entire poetry staff resigned in protest.

In August 2018, I received an interview request from a law firm hired by the Pulitzer Prize Board to investigate whether The Author should retain his membership on the board of directors. The law firm invited me to a contemporary office building in downtown Los Angeles, and we sat in a super-modern conference room, walled in floor-to-ceiling windows. One of the lawyers, a young white woman around my age, told me that she recognized the area code in my phone number. We were both from the same region in Pennsylvania, she said with a disarming smile. My husband sat silently at the conference table as I reenacted my encounter with The Author for the room of attorneys. I remember their inscrutable grins, framed by a panorama of the LA skyline, granite mountains, sunshine, and deep blue skies. My body felt incredibly heavy, it was too much to even cry.

The summer after Sydney, while finishing up my book tour, I was contacted by a reporter at *The Boston Globe.* I vaguely registered her name when my editor told me, on a visit to New York, that she had called their office. She had emailed me a while back asking for comment. When I returned home to Los Angeles, I finally called her back.

I felt that something was off fairly early into the conversation, that I was being asked to defend myself when I hadn't done anything wrong. All I'd done was tell the truth. But I wasn't wary enough.

A few weeks later, I was sent the published article on my phone. After I started reading it, I immediately broke down. My husband, my dog, and I were living in a straw-bale house in the middle of the Sonoran desert. We were broke. My husband was in a deep depression and couldn't work; we were loaded with debt and surviving on my adjunct teaching and freelance income.

The article was framed around an interview with The Author, which took place in the office of Liberty Square Group, a Boston communications firm specializing in crisis management and "reputation recovery." He insisted he had not bullied us or been sexually inappropriate, and the article framed the episode as a turning point for the Me Too movement, because even though he faced public shaming, he had retained his positions at various institutions after investigations into his behavior had been conducted. The article featured sections dedicated to each of our claims, marked by our photos. He denied that he had kissed me, and the reporter mentioned that he'd provided the emails I'd sent him after the event that made no mention of the kiss. Then it referenced a Columbia professor who encountered me after the event who described me as "delighted, not shaken."

The next day I tweeted about the phone call I'd had weeks

ago with the reporter. On the phone, she'd asked me if he'd kissed me on the mouth or the cheek. To that day I had told no one, outside of close friends and family, what had happened in that stairwell. I realized that she had spoken to The Author. On the phone, I told her I didn't trust her.

"I don't trust you either!" she screamed at me.

We went back and forth for a while. The whole time, she typed loudly in the background. I asked her to be quiet. "It could have been a friendly greeting," she said of the kiss, and then finally: "I don't want to see you ruin the Me Too movement!" At that point I hung up.

Days after the article was published, I received an email from one of my Columbia professors. She was outraged by the professor quoted in the article. She asked if I had any clue as to who it was and I could only think of one professor I'd invited to the event. He had always been kind to me and I didn't think he was capable of that type of betrayal, but I remembered that he knew The Author. I had no idea who to trust anymore. I was reassured when she told me that she'd raise the issue with the other faculty. I waited hopefully for a reply from her, but it never came.

Several Twitter users harassed the four of us on a daily basis and also targeted my husband. They called us liars, called for The Author to sue us, and tweeted at our employers and friends. One of them phoned my agent's office. Another changed their handle and display name to the sci-fi writer's father's name shortly after he died.

One account in particular dogged us with particularly barbed insults. The account changed handles frequently and seemed to have inside knowledge of the literary world. It tweeted a picture of the back cover of my book and named some of the authors who had written endorsements. "Which one of you lied and told Zinzi Clemmons she could write?" it wrote. "Just words on a page, with pseudo-characters that couldn't be brought to life. Bad for a hater that called [The Author] talentless." "Did [The Author] decline to blurb your book," it wrote. "What's at the root of your despicable behavior for the last 4 months?"

The account also tweeted the name of the professor I'd given as possibly the Columbia professor in *The Boston Globe* article. I'd shared his name with no one else. "According to @zinziclemmons it was [Professor's name] who was the Columbia professor. He was also the one who started the preemptive rumor about [#TheAuthor's] essay. Dude has to be a literary clown." The Twitter account had to have been connected to Columbia faculty. I could see no other reason for it. Later, the sci-fi writer received multiple anonymous tips saying the account was run by The Author. The sci-fi writer wrote to the journalist who made this accusation.

"Can you tell me why you think it's him?" the sci-fi writer asked.

"I'm a journalist with excellent sources," she replied.

A few months after I was interviewed by the Pulitzer Board's lawyers, they announced the result of their investigation: "The review did not find evidence warranting removal of [The Author] from the Board. Accordingly, after full discussion and consideration by the members, [The Author] will be welcomed to resume his full duties as a Board member and to fulfill his term."

No details were given as to what kinds of behavior would warrant removal. To the outside world, he had been cleared of any wrongdoing.

A letter was published in The Author's support in *The Chronicle of Higher Education*, signed by prominent women writers and scholars. It included one of my former mentors and some friends and associates of the other women. A counter letter was written in our support. Some friends embraced me; others disappeared. I gained Twitter followers. Some career connections went dead. Many other times, I was too afraid to reach out, fearing what rejection might mean.

I was a liar, people said. I was out for attention. I was petulant, naive, crazy. I repeated these words in my mind for weeks, months sometimes. I tried them on in the mirror, regarded them from different angles to see if they fit. I feared that I had ruined a cause that I believed in. I was to blame for all of it, and slowly I turned the hatred of others inward, on myself.

It all hurt so much that I stopped writing and stopped thinking about publishing. My career, which was taking off when I went public, largely stalled. I hid myself away just hoping it would end.

In the fall of 2018, I sat in the waiting room of a psychiatric clinic, where I filled out a diagnostic survey on an iPad handed to me by a receptionist. When it asked if I'd thought about harming myself, I pressed yes. When it asked if I thought I'd be better off dead, I pressed yes.

I had a quick intake with a warm woman who told me that the

provider's resources were stretched thin, but they would be able to make room for me. She looked at me softly; I could tell she took pity on me. She recommended that I look up self-help videos on YouTube and gave me the name of a therapist in Burbank.

Diagnosis: Major Depressive Disorder

Post-Traumatic Stress Disorder

I learned that I had been experiencing classic PTSD symptoms for months, from intrusive thoughts to disassociation, the feeling that I was floating outside of my own body. Some parts of me came back together in these months, but it took a huge toll on my life. Even though he supported me immensely during this time, the damage to my relationship with my husband was tremendous. I lost contact with friends and pushed others away in anticipation of them hurting me. These were the dark times. While it was happening, I was completely unsure that I would emerge from it.

I thought I had carefully packaged the sexual assault from 2013 and shoved it far enough inside me to not be felt, but eventually, I confronted it in therapy. What happened to me was assault. I was kissed and groped and fondled when I didn't want to be. I tried to say no.

I was too drunk to even know what was happening. I was assaulted and almost raped.

I was bullied by The Author. He kissed me without my consent. I was made into a sexual object. I was blamed. I was disbelieved. I was retaliated against.

My therapist told me that PTSD has secondary determinants

and is hugely subject to what happens in the immediate aftermath of the trauma, which affects how you process the event. Take a horrific car crash. Studies have shown that if there is someone in the car who survives along with you, who is there to talk you through it, you are less likely to develop PTSD. On the other hand, if you are alone for a long time and in constant fear that you will die, you are more likely to develop symptoms. If you are lucky enough to have access to therapy and a support system that will acknowledge your pain and help you through it, the chances are even lower, and over time you will heal.

On Facebook, I noticed that the tone of my aunts' and cousins' posts in South Africa started to change dramatically. Normally irreverent, casual, they became frustrated, militant even. They spoke about how difficult it was to be a woman, about being abused, assaulted, and ignored. My aunties—who normally blanched at such talk—liked their messages. They posted encouraging, defiant replies.

I started to see a name: Uyinene. It sounded like one of my favorite words, *ululate*, which I love for how it echoes the specific cries of South African women at celebrations and funerals—the sharp, high-pitched wailing, sung from deep in the breast of women I love. From the pictures I saw posted online, Uyinene was striking, gorgeous, bursting with youth. A big smile, beautiful round features, and glowing skin. She was hip, stylish, and unmistakably African. My mind superimposed the thought of what was done to her. It was difficult to reconcile the two.

I felt the stirring of joy, felt the pang of painful memories not yet healed. Even though we were separated by geography and culture, nation and privilege, we were together. I hesitated when I felt my heart soar, but after a while I allowed myself to feel hope.

In the final months of her life, my mother was preparing for a federal review of her program at work that would determine if it would regain federal funding and thus if thousands of low-income children in Philadelphia would have access to free day care, meals, and early education. She was so busy and had such a strong sense of responsibility for her work that she decided to forgo her treatments in order to complete her task. She chose the well-being of those children, many of whom she would never meet, over her own life.

In subsequent years, I would be contacted three more times for an article like the one published in *The Boston Globe*, by The Author's former supervisor at a literary magazine. Twice the article was killed after I contacted the editors at each outlet and successfully appealed to the piece's editors' journalistic ethics—I pointed out, simply, that they could not publish the truth if they did not know the entire story. I offered to work with them on an exposé starting with the dozens of accounts we'd collected. Two outlets refused to publish the editor's article, but eventually another one did.

Each time this happened, I would be sent into a spiral of depression that would sometimes last for weeks. I would feel the progress I'd made wind back and felt I was right back where I started.

In November 2022, while three months pregnant, I was contacted by Ben Smith, a politics reporter at *Semafor.* He had obtained the report from the Pulitzer Prize Board that contained the testimony I gave in Los Angeles. I was never notified by the Pulitzer board of the contents of this report, nor that it would be released.

As I had with the other articles, I spoke to Smith off the record. I told him about The Author's initial statement where he seemingly admitted to wrongdoing. About the Berkeley workshop alumni's open letter. The dozens of leads we'd collected. He was unaware of all of it.

"So you're protecting other people?" he asked. I told him I was.

He seemed stunned. "How should I write about this?" he asked sincerely. I leaned on my professional expertise. If he wasn't willing to follow the leads, he *shouldn't* write about it, I told him. He seemed to absorb it. He seemed to like me. Respect me. He thanked me for the conversation. When I hung up the phone, I felt I'd made him see things from my perspective. I had hope the article wouldn't go forward, but the piece was published the next day with no mention of anything I'd told him. Just like the *Boston Globe* article, this one also centered on an interview with The Author; my perspective, and those of the other people he'd harmed, were completely shut out of the narrative.

The depression came, but this time I recovered more quickly. I had my baby to think about, I knew I had to stay strong for him. My pregnant body couldn't physically handle the stress I'd gone through in earlier years.

A few months later, my son was born totally healthy, ten wiggly fingers and toes, sparkling brown eyes. He was everything I dreamed of, and he helped dull the pain of what had happened to me. Or maybe I made myself forget in order to love him.

I started to heal. I could talk about what happened without getting worked up. I could even sometimes joke about it. I started to write again. I immersed myself in teaching, the small joys of normal life, far away from industry parties and reporters and gossip. I focused on writing projects that took me in new directions. We bought a house. I made new friends. I began to put what happened behind me.

Naturally, given everything I went through, at times I wished I'd never spoken up. In the 2020s, the pendulum swung backward. The movement had gone too far, many said. Where was due process for the accused? Their rights were being infringed. Maybe we *shouldn't* believe women.

The powerful banked high-profile victories against their accusers. I closely followed several cases with trepidation and anxiety: the overturning of Bill Cosby's conviction in 2021; the show trial of Amber Heard in 2022; Stephen Elliott's settlement with Moira Donegan in 2023. There were tremendous gains, for sure, but that progress always felt fragile, and I feared what these legal victories—pyrrhic though they were—portended.

The reelection of Donald Trump seemed likely to set back the gains of Me Too considerably. But, in my opinion, that has not been so. Allegations of sexual misconduct against Pete Hegseth garnered serious publicity during his confirmation hearing for secretary of defense and fully thwarted Matt Gaetz's nomination for attorney general. Allegations of sexual misconduct—even in those cases—are taken more seriously than in the past, and often as fact. Believing victims is not the realm of the far right—they have even taken the incredible step to minimize these crimes as insignificant.

In the center-left mainstream, the accused still maintain an incredibly high standard to face consequences to their reputation, career, and material wealth. Such debates usually take place in the intellectual silos of Twitter, op-ed pages, and academic journals, which falsely imagine their sole power over any accuser's fate. It is always up to the public to decide who they listen to, read, and watch and which products they consume. No single accuser, academic, or article holds the power to determine anyone's artistic relevance, or even whether they can make money. The world is simply too big, and as has been proven over and over by "canceled" public figures who go on to lucrative second acts, there are unlimited audiences if only one has the ingenuity to find them.

Critiques of Me Too misidentify it as an organized political movement rather than a spontaneous outpouring of victims' stories, which, together, accumulated power. Me Too has merely validated and circulated information that in the past was confined to rumor and whisper network. Contrary to the tortured arguments of the *Harper's* Letter and other reactionaries, Me Too and "cancel culture" together constitute one of the most important democraticizing free speech movements in history.

The moral panics around Me Too and cancel culture are reactions to the rapid dispersal of power aided by demographic shifts, the democratization of information via technology, and the increasing power of women. Thanks to these advances, the powerful are now subject to the same random fluctuations that the disempowered have always been. For every famous actor or CEO taken down by sexual misconduct allegations, there are countless workers fired for rejecting their boss's advances.

Like many other political issues, those for and against these movements tend to fall along the generational divide and amount to a struggle over resources. The younger generations face a future determined by climate change, with diminished voting rights, bodily autonomy, and financial security. Millennials, having come of age in two major economic downturns, have the least amount of wealth so far in history, waiting to be outdone by Generations Z through Beta. On the other side of this divide sit those with stock portfolios, 401(k)s, and real estate. They own the world and have left increasingly little for the young; they have everything to lose and know we are starving. Of course we are angry.

If previous eras were defined by the death of God and the death of the author, Me Too inaugurates the death of the idol. The democratization of media has meant that everyone suffers intense scrutiny, and under such scrutiny, everyone is revealed as human. This is a positive development, and as is common with all societal adjustments, it is painful at first. Over time, society will absorb these shocks and come to recognize it as forward movement.

That said, I remain critical of the failings of this so-called Me Too movement, which largely coincide with those of mainstream feminism—for centering rich, white cis-hetero women and failing to adequately address the experiences of people of color, the working class, trans and nonbinary people, and the poor. Predictably, justice has been disproportionately meted out to the privileged, and far too many without power have not been lifted. In my opinion, more advocacy and writing should be done about gig and service-industry workers than film actors and even authors.

But I am deeply satisfied that, in the wider world, things are better than they were before. More people, like me, have been empowered to speak, and more often than in the past, they do not face total erasure.

Was it worth it? I have sat with this question often while surveying the emotional wreckage of the past decade of my life. I think of where I might be if I'd stayed quiet. But then I remember myself as a graduate student in my twenties, full of ambition and hope, talent and promise, and my small, abiding belief in fairness. I ask myself: Was I right?

Hell, yes!

A PEOPLE WITHOUT A NATION

When our fears have all been serialized, our creativity censured, our ideas "marketplaced," our rights sold, our intelligence sloganized, our strength downsized, our privacy auctioned; when the theatricality, the entertainment value, the marketing of life is complete, we will find ourselves living not in a nation but in a consortium of industries, and wholly unintelligible to ourselves except for what we see as through a screen darkly.

—Toni Morrison, "Racism and Fascism," from the 1995 speech at Howard University

Bigger, you're going to die. And if you die, die free.

—Richard Wright, *Native Son*

You could have called me an Afropessimist for much of my life. I was born in 1985, and in 1986 I was on a plane to Johannesburg, against the advice of the US government and the good sense of my parents' friends. South Africa was on the brink then, feeling the impact of international boycotts and lurching toward independence. Violence spiraled. One of my earliest memories is watching my uncle reach into the glove compartment of his parked truck and seeing a handgun tumble forth, my sudden awareness of its gravity, literal and atmospheric, as it landed in his hand from atop a stack of papers. There was the constant clanking of metal bars, the ever-higher walls topped by barbed wire, everyday markers of brutality meant to keep the races apart.

In suburban Pennsylvania, another form of apartheid was present. My black classmates lived in segregated, lower-income neighborhoods and took remedial classes, while white children lived in big houses and populated honors classes. There were quiet limits placed on black children and families, policed by our white counterparts. I was one of very few black children who lived in a white neighborhood and took honors classes, for which I was rewarded with the gifts of loneliness and alienation. In college, I read critical theory and Frantz Fanon and felt mired in a position in contrast to my white peers. I saw everything through the veil of my blackness, retreated into it and felt comfort only there.

I was, however, brought up differently. My parents met in Botswana, where my father went after college. My mother was still in university and had come to Gaborone with an ANC-sympathizing student group. My father was one of the first Americans she'd ever met. In their first conversation, she relayed to him the brutality of the political situation that was, at that time, kept from the Western press.

In this way, politics was foundational to the way they met. For black people who came of age during the 1960s, the question of where one stood was impossible to avoid. They read anti-colonial black writers like Fanon and Walter Rodney. Like many people of their age and political persuasion, they were especially drawn to the teachings of Steve Biko.

In "Black Consciousness and the Quest for True Humanity," Biko laid out the tenets of Black Consciousness, which identified white racism as the true cause of apartheid—not segregation, as white liberals had diagnosed it. The only force that could counter white racism, Biko said, was radical black solidarity, which extended to all nonwhite groups.

> Blacks must sit as one big unit and no fragmentation and distraction from the main stream of events must be allowed. Hence we must resist the attempts by the protagonists of "separate development" to fragment our approach. We are oppressed not as individuals, not as Zulus, Xhosas, Vendas or Indians. We are oppressed because we are Black. We must use that very concept to unite ourselves and to respond as a cohesive group. We must cling to each other with a tenacity that must shock the perpetrators of evil.

Even though my parents came from different parts of the world and had what some would call mixed heritage, their idea of blackness was large enough to encompass all of us. They taught us a loving, radical blackness that connected us with my father's Trinidadian family and our friends in the ghettos of Philadelphia.

In 2014, while at an artist colony in New Hampshire, this all-white place under a blanket of white snow (where, during my eight-week stay, I was one of three black artists in residence), I struck up a friendship with a white performance artist from the Bay Area. One day at dinner he told me that his intellectual focus du jour was Afropessimism and without a hint of irony proceeded to explain the discourse to me in detail. It struck me as both contrived and familiar. Black people are natural pessimists, with good reason, a response to the unfair ways in which we've been treated. I walked away thinking of Afropessimism as another obscure academic formulation and didn't think about it much for some time after that.

Afropessimism encompasses a broad range of academic discourse and scholarship. In its simplest terms, it sees blackness as an abstract position (think the Marxist conception of "the worker," the feminist "woman," or the postcolonial "native") equal to that of a slave and subject to unique forms of violence (deemed, familiarly, "antiblack" violence), thereby suggesting that genuine cross-racial identification is impossible. In popular discourse, Afropessimism has taken on a simplified definition that basically amounts to nihilism toward the position of blacks in society. Increasingly, the term is used loosely as a signifier attached to much of the contemporary discourse on blackness, which, unlike the radical uplift of previous decades, is suffused with the tragedy of black people's position in America: with achievement gaps, police violence, mass incarceration, maternal mortality, and on and on.

Orlando Patterson, whose work is hugely foundational to Afropessimist discourse (but who does not, himself, identify as part of it) wrote in 1972:

> The Blacks of the Americas now face a historic choice. To survive, they must abandon their search for a past, must indeed recognize that they lack all claims to a distinctive cultural heritage, and that the path ahead lies not in myth making and in historical reconstruction, which are always doomed to failure, but in accepting

> the epic challenge of their reality. Black Americans can be the first group in the history of mankind who transcend the confines and grip of a cultural heritage, and in so doing, they can become the most truly modern of all peoples—a people who feel no need for a nation, a past, or a particularistic culture, but whose style of life will be a rational and continually changing adaptation to the exigencies of survival, at the highest possible level of existence.

Saidiya Hartman, one of the most prominent black scholars working today and lesser known for her association with Afropessimism, opened her 2016 essay "The Belly of the World: A Note on Black Women's Labors," invoking Édouard Glissant: "The slave ship is a womb/abyss." The essay extends Glissant's gendered metaphor of the slave ship in order to explore the contributions and commodifications of black women's bodies since slavery. "This boat is a womb, a womb abyss," writes Glissant in "The Open Boat." "It generates the clamor of your protests; it also produces all the coming unanimity. Although you are alone in this suffering, you share in the unknown with others whom you have yet to know." We are "born on the water"—the title of Nikole Hannah-Jones's children's book under the *1619 Project* banner. These texts notably locate the birthplace of blackness on the slave route, necessarily separating it from the diaspora.

These contributions are important. The singularity of black American identity is undeniable, and the unique disadvantages dealt to American descendants of slavery cannot be overstated.

The reclamation of slavery into a narrative of agency and empowerment is significant. It also directly contradicts the big, loving blackness instilled in me. Where does such fragmentation leave me, a child of Africa and the United States and the Caribbean? Where is my birthplace?

The origin of the term *Afropessimism* can be traced to a 2003 interview between Frank Wilderson and Saidiya Hartman, his mentor, occasioned by a discussion of the latter's *Scenes of Subjection*. Hartman's intention, and a fundamental aim of her broader work, is to acknowledge the impossibility of imagining the position of the enslaved, an idea that appeals immensely to me as a literary writer but which generated ample criticism as a work of historical scholarship. "In many ways," Hartman said, "what I was trying to do as a cultural historian was to narrate a certain impossibility, to illuminate those practices that speak to the limits of most available narratives to explain the position of the enslaved. On one hand, the slave is the foundation of the national order, and, on the other, the slave occupies the position of the unthought." Affirming the inability to imagine the slave's subjectivity is also a rejection of the ability to incorporate such subjectivities into a national project.

> [Hartman]—What then does this language—the given language of freedom—enable? And once you realize its limits and begin to see its inexorable investment in certain notions of the subject and subjection, then that lan-

> guage of freedom no longer becomes that which rescues the slave from his or her former condition, but the site of the re-elaboration of that condition, rather than its transformation.
>
> [Wilderson]—This is one of the reasons why your book has been called "pessimistic."

In the aftermath of the 2020 racial uprisings, "Afropessimism" was uttered on podcasts, in blog posts, and in comic strips. It is used to refer to any number of writers, individuals, television shows, political figures, and storylines. More and more people outside of academia define themselves as Afropessimists—or some referential variant—sometimes ironically, sometimes completely sincerely.

"Why is anti-Black violence not a form of racist hatred but the *genome* of Human renewal," Frank Wilderson asks in his breakthrough 2020 memoir *Afropessimism*, "a therapeutic balm that the Human race needs to know and heal itself? . . . Why must the world find its nourishment in Black flesh?" In 2020, *The New York Times* decried: CALL IT WHAT IT IS: ANTIBLACKNESS, with its subhead: WHEN BLACK PEOPLE ARE KILLED BY THE POLICE, "RACISM" ISN'T THE RIGHT WORD. And even *Forbes* ran a primer on RECOGNIZING AND DISMANTLING YOUR ANTIBLACKNESS.

In a review of Ta-Nehisi Coates's *We Were Eight Years in Power*, Darryl Pinckney, identifying similarity between Coates and Wilderson, poses, "Maybe [Afropessimism is] another name for something that has been around in black culture for a while." In "On Afropessimism," Jesse McCarthy argues that, taken together, this growing tendency toward Afropessimism may be designated a historical "mood":

> Like the related terms "affect" or Raymond Williams's "structure of feeling," a "mood" is notoriously difficult to analyze. We grasp it only indirectly, like the sounds from a party in the building next door. It circulates in the hyperactive synapses of our society where different registers of language agglutinate into shorthands and neologisms—"doomscrolling," "cancelled," "triggered," "killing it," "I'm dead"—that suggest some of it just by association. Every once in a while, a handle comes along that electrifies a whole swath of experiences at once, moments of rupture when a philosophy, a political slogan, or even a bit of jargon throws the table over, gathering all those affective undercurrents under a single collectively recognized shout. . . . One can wonder if, retrospectively, Afropessimism, Black Lives Matter, and the Obama presidency will be similarly linked.

If we are, as McCarthy suggests, living in an era of Afropessimism, how does one characterize it?

A couple of years ago my father, who is retired and spends much of his time traveling, brought me a gift from one of his trips: a prayer candle that features the figure of James Baldwin where the Virgin Mary or Saint John might appear, his head ringed with a halo of fire, invoking his seminal work *The Fire Next Time.* Believing as I do that it's harmful to worship artists—who, like politicians and movie stars, inevitably show themselves to be human—I nonetheless appreciate the gift. Its implication is obvious: Particularly after the uprisings of 2020, Baldwin is perhaps the closest thing our culture has to a prophet.

It's surprising, then, how little the contentious event that launched Baldwin's career is remarked upon: his pugilistic critique of his mentor Richard Wright's masterpiece *Native Son.* In "Everybody's Protest Novel," Baldwin dismissed Wright as a "pamphleteer," incapable of the kind of nuance required of real literature. "Sentimentality, the ostentatious parading of excessive and spurious emotion," Baldwin proclaimed, "is the mark of dishonesty, the inability to feel; the wet eyes of the sentimentalist betray his aversion to experience, his fear of life, his arid heart; and it is always, therefore, the signal of secret and violent inhumanity, the mask of cruelty."

At first, I admired the courage and ambition Baldwin displayed in this act of rebellion against Wright, and it connected to my own distrust of older generations. I have always relished open discourse, especially among black writers, and placed their feud in the long tradition of debate that began with W. E. B. Du Bois and Booker T. Washington, which sparked countless moments of discovery and insight in black intellectual thought.

In the early 1940s, James Baldwin moved from his home in Harlem to Greenwich Village, and into the heart of New York's avant-garde literary scene. He found a job at Calypso Restaurant, an integrated hangout where he would rub elbows with the city's black glitterati. It was around this time that he met Richard Wright, who arranged a publishing deal for his first book, though it never came to fruition. He also met the white editors of several influential periodicals—*The New Leader*, *Commentary*, and *Partisan Review*—and began writing reviews for them, becoming one of the first black writers to address questions of race openly in their pages.

"Everybody's Protest Novel" was one of several essays written by Baldwin in the early part of his career that critiqued social realist literature. His 1947 review of Chester Himes's *Lonely Crusade* makes his treatment of Wright seem gentle in comparison. Himes, another avowed Marxist, would become friends with Baldwin and Wright in Paris. In his review, Baldwin wrote that Himes "seems capable of some of the worst writing this side of the Atlantic."

Baldwin's "Everybody's Protest Novel" is representative of a key argument in literature at that time that was itself an avatar for the geopolitical battle between democratic liberalism and Soviet-style Marxism, presaging the central conflict of the coming Cold War. As publications, *The New Leader* and *Partisan Review* established themselves in opposition to the Communist Party's Popular Front campaign to capture liberal intellectuals. Famously, *Partisan Review* was covertly funded by the CIA during the 1950s and 1960s. Baldwin's distaste for social realism and protest literature in favor of avant-garde ideals of individuality and "complexity" were sentiments widely held among the white New York intellectual establishment at that time. Though "Everybody's Protest Novel" was originally published by the French journal *Zen*, it later appeared in *Partisan Review* and finally in *Perspectives USA*, a magazine whose mission was "to woo European intellectuals to the side of freedom."

With "Everybody's Protest Novel," Baldwin permanently shifted public opinion in his favor and eventually completely eclipsed his mentor. Baldwin, not Wright, has taken the place of foremost public black intellectual, so much so that it is hard to find mainstream writing on Wright—no matter how positive—that isn't filtered through Baldwin's criticism. In 2019, HBO released a new adaptation of *Native Son*, and in 2021, a previously unpublished novel by Wright, *The Man Who Lived Underground*, was finally printed, occasioning a new wave of writing on the author, almost all of which comports with Baldwin's critique. The 2019 film is a facile adaptation of Wright's masterpiece toned down for the woke era. The film recasts Bigger Thomas as a well-meaning but misunderstood middle-class young man, completely obviating Wright's class-based critique of segregated Chicago. The film garnered a host of negative reviews (and a measly 60 percent rating on Rotten Tomatoes) and led *The New Yorker* to proclaim that it "has reached the limit of what the text has left to offer." Writing in *The Atlantic*, Imani Perry expresses the most sympathetic view. "Now that I've read *The Man Who Lived Underground*," Perry wrote, "I'm even more convinced that Wright deserves to be looked at with fresh eyes."

Baldwin's critique of Bigger Thomas as "categorization alone"—i.e., stereotype—is accepted far too easily. Bigger Thomas is a violent rapist, thieving, hateful, and uncaring—all traits associated with stereotypes of African Americans—but a stereotype he is not. On the contrary, Wright carefully renders his psychology over the course of the novel so that we understand intimately what drives him to kill, to rape, and in the end, to show no remorse for his crimes. A rereading reveals that almost a century later, Bigger Thomas remains one of the most enduring characters in literature.

As most fictional characters are, Thomas was an amalgamation of real people Wright encountered in his life under Jim Crow. The name Bigger is a portmanteau of "bad nigger"—which Wright nicknamed one of these men who bullied his way into the cinema where Wright worked as a ticket taker without paying. "'I'd point into the darkened theater and say: 'Bigger's in there.' 'Did he pay?' the proprietor would ask. 'No, sir,' I'd answer." Wright held a complicated respect for these characters:

> The Bigger Thomases were the only Negroes I know of who consistently violated the Jim Crow laws of the South and got away with it, at least for a sweet brief spell. Eventually, the whites who restricted their lives made them pay a terrible price. They were shot, hanged, maimed, lynched, and generally hounded until they were either dead or their spirits broken.

Good characters contain negative and redeeming traits and show themselves as a product of the particular forces of their home environment. In Bigger, Wright created a fully formed avatar of the ravages of Jim Crow, a grotesque yet realistic vision of the limits of freedom under the extreme repression of the racist state. Thomas was Wright's attempt to imagine what compelled human beings to acts of violence, recognizing that such individuals were powering fascist movements during the pre–World War II era. He wrote:

> From far away Nazi Germany and old Russia had come to me items of knowledge that told me that certain modern experiences were creating types of personalities whose existence ignored racial and national lines of demarcation . . . these personalities were mainly imposed upon men and women living in a world whose fundamental assumptions could no longer be taken for granted: a world ridden with national and class strife; a world whose metaphysical meanings had vanished; a world in which God no longer existed as a daily focal point of men's lives; a world in which men could no longer retain their faith in an ultimate hereafter. It was a highly geared world whose nature was conflict and action, a world whose limited area and vision imperiously urged men to satisfy their organisms, a world that existed on a plane of animal sensation alone.

Facing a global resurgence in fascism, when mass shootings have become an everyday occurrence, where police murders and hate killings are broadcast on personal devices like episodes of sitcoms, today's world looks a lot like the one Wright described almost a century ago. Bigger Thomas provides a window into the psychology of the school shooter, the serial rapist, and the white supremacist—whom we ignore at our own peril.

Soon after I graduated from college, the economy crashed. I remember the horror of watching the stock market tick lower every day, seeing lives collapse all around and not knowing if mine would be next. America was declared "post-racial," but in fact some black people got richer while the majority got poorer. That included me. I left my first job in book publishing for graduate school, racked up thousands more in debt, and emerged unemployed. The economy supposedly rebounded, but no one around me seemed to. I married a man whose half-white family lived on a razor's edge, and we moved to one of America's left-behind places where there were no jobs, no money, and little to do. For the first time in my life, I was surrounded by white poverty, and my old math was scrambled. Afropessimism faded in me. I no longer felt isolated in my blackness because I was connected to others in struggle.

In its belief in the primacy of antiblack racism, Afropessimist discourse tends to relegate other concerns—such as class, gender, and nationality—to secondary status. This often puts Afropessimists at odds with other disciplines that view these concerns as primary or equal—postcolonial scholars, historians, and most ardently, Marxist scholars, who view racism in material terms and often as a product of capitalism. Taking the broader scholarship of Afropessimism in view, this slippage seems integral—

and perhaps intentional—to a worldview that is predicated on the continuity of the black position over time.

Cedric J. Robinson's *Black Marxism: The Making of the Black Radical Tradition*—a landmark text for Black Studies, radicals, and activists from the ANC through Black Lives Matter—seemingly unites these views in its critique of classic Marxism. Robinson popularized the term "racial capitalism," the understanding of racism as a historically defined system with origins in feudal Europe, which served to organize and expand the enterprise of capitalism.

Robinson devotes an entire chapter to Wright, whose writing, alongside that of C. L. R. James and W. E. B. Du Bois, he viewed as "a first step toward the creation of an intellectual legacy that would complement the historical force of Black struggle." Published in 1984, Robinson's appraisal of Wright's legacy also begins with Baldwin's attack on Wright—alongside that of his other mentee, Ralph Ellison, and others—but he concludes that the impact of Wright's work, in the end, outshone his critics. "He was never merely a 'racial novelist,' a 'protest writer,' or a 'literary rebel' . . . ," Robinson wrote, "His arena was the totality of Western civilization and its constitutive elements. . . . His work thus constituted an inquiry."

It is useful to note the demarcation of Afropessimism, because it marks a primary point of struggle in black liberation. By this I do not mean the conflict between racial pessimism and optimism (the conservative belief that things aren't that bad if only we pick ourselves up by our bootstraps). Black people have plenty of reason to be pessimistic, even nihilistic. The rift I wish to highlight is between the Marxist view of race as a tool of capitalism, a means to the end of white sovereignty, and the liberal view of racism as a permanent, defining feature of society. Underlying much of the works of Wilderson, Baldwin, Coates, and many of today's mainstream black writers is the belief that racism is the primary, permanent distorting feature of society—and thus the only way for it to be destroyed would be for our paradigm as we know it to come to an end. Here is Wilderson:

> But getting rid of social death doesn't mean on the other side having Black existence that is whole. On the other side, it means something more catastrophic and renewing, which is having no Black existence because there will be no Black people. And having no Human existence, because there will be no Humans. There will be sentient beings who are on the cusp of a new episteme.

In *Native Son*, the fates of Bigger and the novel's white Communist characters, Jan and Max, are linked—first by happenstance and later by choice. Though Bigger initially tries to frame Jan for his crimes, Jan forgives him and then supplies him with Max as his defense lawyer. This selfless act is contrasted with the Dalton family's philanthropy—a fig leaf for its segregated real estate enterprise, where they charge Negroes exorbitant rents for the decaying, rat-infested apartments that populate the Black Belt. It is the character of Max who delivers a twenty-page-long soliloquy during the trial, capturing the horrors of the conditions that nurtured Bigger. In this moment, Max—a Jewish

Communist—channels Bigger's thoughts and life experience, and those of Wright:

> Multiply Bigger Thomas twelve million times . . . and you have the psychology of the Negro people. . . . Taken collectively, they are not simply twelve million people; in reality they constitute a separate nation, stunted, stripped, and held captive *within* this nation, devoid of political, social, economic, and property rights.

Black leaders have often paid the ultimate price while seeking cross-racial coalitions. This was true of both Malcolm X and Martin Luther King Jr. at the time of their deaths; of the Black Panthers when they were infiltrated by the CIA; and of Richard Wright at the height of his career. Wright's work was prolifically censored, and after the success of *Native Son*, which sold 250,000 copies within weeks of publication, his publisher rejected its follow-up, *The Man Who Lived Underground*, which remained unpublished for nearly a century. Shortly before self-exiling to France, Wright renounced communism and embraced black nationalism. He died at age fifty-two under mysterious circumstances; his family and friends have suggested CIA involvement.

Wright fought valiantly against a mainstream that sought to suppress the material empowerment of impoverished Americans, and for that he remains one of the most courageous writers of all time. Baldwin, later in his career, was also one of them, as he joined with the Civil Rights Movement and became increasingly radical himself. Though his aesthetics may go in and out of fashion, Wright's technical skill in his ability to marshal tension, feeling, and character to indelible effect is unmatched. The legacy of Richard Wright represents the success of the liberal agenda in suppressing the black radical tradition. Baldwin's criticism of Wright—promoted by white liberal forces who sought to destroy the radical Wright—marked a crucial encounter between these viewpoints. The litigation of this struggle continues.

An Afropessimist narrative took hold in the aftermath of the 2016 presidential election. This narrative, repeated by mainstream pundits, op-ed writers, and Twitter users, held that racism was the sole cause of Donald Trump's election. This narrative was loudly countered by reductive leftists who held that it was the economy, stupid, that drove disaffected white voters to vote for Trump. A small, quieter group asserted that such an outcome couldn't be distilled to one single factor and instead argued for nuance. Finding myself in the latter group, I unwisely advertised my opinion online and soon found myself embroiled in a debate with a writer who told me that he couldn't agree with any analysis of the election that didn't hold antiblack racism as its central cause. We sparred online over the course of several hours with increasing acrimony. The next morning, I awoke to an apology in my email inbox. We haven't spoken since.

Over the course of the next several years, headline after headline repudiated my stance, culminating in an analysis of American National Election Studies pre- and post-2016 election survey by researchers Sean McElwee and Jason McDaniel. The study, confidently touted by mainstream outlets as incontrovertible proof that racism—*not* economic anxiety—caused the 2016 outcome, asked respondents a series of questions to gauge racial animus, anti-immigration sentiment, and "black influence animosity" (the belief that the US government favors black people). It found that Republican voters had higher levels of racial animus than economic anxiety. The study does not account for the sizable portion of the electorate that abstained from the election, which was overwhelmingly younger, less affluent, and more likely to vote Democratic. This bloc of nonvoters abstained in numbers large enough to cause formerly Democratic-voting states such as Wisconsin, Michigan, and Pennsylvania to swing to the Republican Party.

Donald Trump's overt racism awoke liberal America from the post-racial slumber of the Obama years. Hate groups, which had been on the rise since early in Obama's term, became a preoccupation of mainstream news. Headlines proclaimed racism to be alive and well. In the days after Trump's election, I received sincere apologies from white acquaintances for the election result. All of a sudden, white American liberals became very concerned with the issue of racism in the United States.

Soon, a cottage industry devoted to educating white people about racism emerged. Figureheads such as Robin DiAngelo and Ibram X. Kendi made millions touting liberal anti-racist messages. During this time, *The New York Times*'s *1619 Project* found a receptive audience in white people more open than usual to critiques of racism and black readers unused to such high-profile race-based critiques of American history. For all of the fanfare and political furor it produced, it's jarring to remember that *The 1619 Project* was nothing more than a special issue of a mainstream newsmagazine featuring solid though far from revolutionary articles celebrating black contributions to culture and history—in all likelihood commissioned to address its lack of coverage of black subjects.

Much like the work of Coates, these projects correctly diagnose the racism in our society, but they fall short of Wright's vision, outlined in "Blueprint for Negro Writing," for a literature of engagement among writers of all races that does not just critique but endeavors "to ask questions, to theorize, to speculate, to wonder out of what materials can a human world be built."

I remember watching the Minneapolis 3rd Precinct building burn on May 28, 2020, protesters silhouetted against a wall of flame—euphoric, defiant. A living symbol of the racist state crumbled before my eyes, and for the next few days, as I saw young people gather, destroy, and build with one another in the streets it felt like anything was possible. A new world was about to be born.

While 2020 brought greater visibility and strength to black liberation movements, the black elite was just as easily co-opted. The early 2020s brought us a generation of well-compensated black luminaries. We achieved more black representation in boardrooms, in university administrations, on television screens, and in politics. Hired for a tenure-track job at the University of California in 2021, I include myself in this list. More and more, this growing representation has become synonymous with black progress. I would suggest *black excellence* is a companion term, not an antonym, to Afropessimism. While the gains of this era may portend genuine progress, they remain to trickle down to the lives of most black people.

Instead of racial uplift, we got sensitivity training and statements of solidarity. Amazon believes Black Lives Matter. Check out the Black Experience curated by Netflix. In a stunning denouement, grassroots organizers, activists, and voters from former Republicans to far leftists banded together in a feat of historical will to elect an architect of mass incarceration as president. The poor got poorer and a new generation of black millionaires were minted.

What began as a hopeful rebellion against the racialized violence of the police state, a primal scream against the vicissitudes of capitalism that left millions to choose between death by disease and death by hunger, ended in the ideological cul-de-sac of nihilism, a shape common to Wilderson's and my suburban childhoods.

In his 1984 essay, "On Being White . . . and Other Lies," Baldwin wrote about the shifting nature of whiteness. "White" is not a fixed racial category; rather he reminds us that several ethnic groups—like the Irish and Jewish people—have become white over time, "justifying a totally false identity and . . . what must be called a genocidal history." The power of Baldwin's analysis is limited by him not extending the same mutability to "black" people. This idea is challenged, again, by the diaspora—in much of Africa and parts of the Caribbean—where "black" holds a wholly different meaning than in the United States.

Where is my birthplace?

In a 1995 speech at Howard University, later excerpted and published as "Racism and Fascism," Toni Morrison posits the afflictions of her title as succubus twins:

> Democrats have no unsullied history of egalitarianism. Nor are liberals free of domination agendas. . . . Conservative, moderate, liberal; right, left, hard left, far right; religious, secular, socialist—we must not be blindsided by these Pepsi-Cola, Coca-Cola labels because the genius of fascism is that any political structure can host the virus and virtually any developed country can become a suitable home. Fascism talks ideology, but it is really just marketing—marketing for power.

It is prudent to remain leery of power, no matter its party, flag, or skin color. Witness: The increase in black support for Trump in the 2020 and 2024 elections, and the many supporters of Israel among the black political class.

In this moment of desolation and uncertainty I look to Wright, wondering who will lead us forward.

CODA

In this sleepy college town with tidy parks and neat houses, smiling children ride their bikes to school unescorted. In the afternoon, they rove the streets in cheerful packs, giggling, cavorting; unthreatening, unthreatened.

One spring morning we awake to a dead man on the park bench where he slept every night. We speak, puzzled, to our friends, not yet aware enough to be scared.

Just because we don't have a home and keys that doesn't make us any less of a person.

Then a student is thrown off his bike and stabbed on his way home from the university.

We moved from Lebanon in 2018 . . . , his father says. *We came here hoping for safety.*

The meek shall inherit society's contempt.

Irrigation ditches, railway trenches, and other dark crannies hold clusters of tents, hidden people living lives the exact inverse of its accounted citizens. In the elbow of Second Street, which I pass every day on my way to work, a woman fights off the killer through the nylon of her tent. She is badly injured, but she lives.

We started sleeping in groups . . . We don't want to be alone.

My husband walks the dog and runs to the grocery store while I stay inside, guarding my growing belly from invisible phantoms. On Friday the killer is caught and we exhale. On Saturday we drive to the mountains in the pouring rain to celebrate our freedom. On Sunday we make love and my water breaks and our son arrives. We become a whole different we: a tribe of three, hopeful as ever, our worry replaced, for now, with joy.

We learn that the killer was expelled a week earlier from the university. Years ago, he entered the country from El Salvador as an unaccompanied minor. A standout student, leader, and football player at his high school in the East Oakland ghetto, he dreamed of becoming a doctor.

In jail, he thinks he is still a college student, telling the guards he needs to register for classes next quarter. He's done poorly this year, he admits, but he can still turn things around.

He had said that the devil was talking to him in his dreams, a witness testifies.

He is deemed unfit for trial. The jury hangs. Mercy and justice lock horns.

We observe the cyclical nature of violence, its remarkable ability to reproduce in disparate environments but always finding the same target: the unsheltered.

We need to be protected. We're humans, too.

From parenting books, we learn that love is a rush of chemicals evolved to keep animals from abandoning their young. But when I see my son's smile, feel his new fingers, impossibly small, grasping my shoulder, I ask myself new questions like, Can you build a nation based on love?

ACKNOWLEDGMENTS

This book is the product of eight years in the wilderness from which I sometimes thought I would not return. I am proud to have emerged and am grateful to the individuals and institutions that have sustained me and my work through that time.

Thank you to everyone who read and improved this book: Fred D'Aguiar, Erin Gray, Akua Banful, Jesse McCarthy, Carmen Maria Machado, Monica Byrne, Alisa Rivera, Vera Angela Webster. To my hometown heroes, both named and unnamed: Kathye Petrie, Jeannine Osayande, Amy Beth Sisson, Liza, and Ray. To Butch and family, thank you for opening your hearts and home to me, and for sharing your beautiful stories of Rob. To Dorris, rest in peace.

To Rob Payne, I will never forget you.

Thank you to Ed Keane for years of conversation, and to Grandma Sue, in heaven, for being the most glamorous and willing subject.

Thanks to Jin Auh, Allison Lorentzen, Sonia Gadre, and Emily Fishman for your dedication to this book and my career.

ACKNOWLEDGMENTS

Thanks to my first reader, André, and to Marcel, for making every day joyful. Thank you to Michael Clemmons, Rachel Broudy, Madeleine Lipshie-Williams, and Angela Flournoy.

A hearty middle finger to all the abusers, enablers, censors, Nazis, and conformists. You won't stop us from making a better world.

NOTES

Author's Note

xix **"Who were the first persons":** Orlando Patterson, *Freedom*, vol 1: *Freedom in the Making of Western Culture* (BasicBooks, 1991), 9.

Swan Song for the Republic

7 **"This is not about":** From remarks by Marco Rubio, Secretary of State, regarding the federal immigration case of former Columbia University student Mahmoud Khalil. Suzanne Gamboa, Carmen Sesin, and Alex Tabet, "Rubio's Record Challenging Repressive Regimes Questioned After Academics' Immigration Crackdown," NBC News, March 21, 2025, nbcnews.com/news/latino/rubio-record-questioned-academics-immigration-crackdown-rcna197470.

Chasing Robbie

36 **On July 4, 2016, Robbie:** Rose Quinn, "Remember Me? After Teacher's Murder, 'Nothing Is the Same,'" *The Delaware County Daily Times*, July 4, 2021, delcotimes.com/2021/07/03/remember-me-after-teachers-murder-nothing-is-the-same-2.

38 **Chester Partnership for Safe Neighborhoods:** Alex Rose, "Chester's 2023 Crime Figures Show Continuing Downward Trend," *The Delaware County Daily Times*, January 26, 2024, delcotimes.com/2024/01/26/chesters-2023-crime-figures-show-continuing-downward-trend.

42 **The area now known as Swarthmore:** "History," Swarthmore Borough, accessed August 13, 2025, swarthmorepa.org/913/History.

43 **Today, Swarthmore's population:** "Swarthmore Borough, Pennsylvania," United States Census Bureau, accessed August 14, 2025, data.census.gov/profile/Swarthmore_borough,_Pennsylvania?g=160XX00US4275648.

43 **In 1958, the white Yarrow family:** Sue Carroll Edwards, "Housing Desegregation in a Small Town," *Friends Journal*, February 15, 2012, friendsjournal.org/housing-desegregation-small-town.

49 **The Second World War brought:** Jake Blumgart, "Chester, Pennsylvania," The Encyclopedia of Greater Philadelphia website, accessed August 15, 2025, philadelphiaencyclopedia.org/essays/chester-pennsylvania.

50 **Until this time, Chester public schools:** John M. McLarnon, "'Old Scratchhead' Reconsidered: George Raymond & Civil Rights in Chester, Pennsylvania," *Pennsylvania History* 69, no. 3 (Summer 2002): 308–310.

50 **By the 1960s, Chester:** McLarnon, "'Old Scratchhead' Reconsidered," 312–313.

50 **Chester's schools reflected:** Christopher Mele describes Chester schools in the 1960s as effectively having been resegregated: "public education in Chester in the early 1960s resembled that of fifteen years earlier. . . . With aging infrastructure, poor funding, and overcrowding, school standards and performance continued to decline," Christopher Mele, *Race and the Politics of Deception: The Making of an American City* (NYU Press, 2017), 83.

51 **Over the course of the 1963–64:** Mele, *Race and the Politics of Deception*, 93–95.

51 **The severity of the events:** "African American residents of Chester, PA, demonstrate to end de facto segregation in public schools, 1963–1966," Global Nonviolent Action Database, accessed August 14, 2025, nvdatabase.swarthmore.edu/content/african-american-residents-chester-pa-demonstrate-end-de-facto-segregation-public-schools-19.

52 **Today, Chester schools are being:** Mari A. Schaefer and Caitlin McCabe, "Judge Rejects Wolf Challenge to Charter Funding," *The Philadelphia Inquirer*, August 25, 2015, inquirer.com/philly/education/20150826_Judge_rejects_Wolf_challenge_to_charter_funding.html.

53 **"So much of school segregation":** This essay owes a large debt to the educational reporting of Nikole Hannah-Jones. Her December 19, 2014, report on the segregation of Michael Brown's education in St. Louis, Missouri, provided a touchstone for the work I did in this piece. I found similarly illuminating the probity with which Hannah-Jones questions herself in the search for her daughter's school, informed by years of research into education in the United States. Nikole Hannah-Jones, "Choosing a School for My Daughter in a Segregated City," *The New York Times Magazine,* June 9, 2016, nytimes.com/2016/06/12/magazine/choosing-a-school-for-my-daughter-in-a-segregated-city.html.

54 **Pennsylvania has five hundred:** "Types of Schools," Department of Education Resources, Commonwealth of Pennsylvania website, accessed August 14, 2025, pa.gov/agencies/education/resources/types-of-schools.

55 **"This decision significantly diminished":** Edbuild, "Fault Lines: America's Most Segregating School Borders," viz.edbuild.org/maps/2016/fault-lines.

55 **In 2015, US Secretary of Education:** Kristen A. Graham, "PA's School-Spending Gap Widest in Nation," *The Philadelphia Inquirer*, March 13, 2015, inquirer.com/philly/news/local/20150314_Pa__s_school-spending_gap_widest_in_nation.html.

55 **Ranked forty-fifth in the nation:** "Pennsylvania Drops to 45th in the Nation in State Funding for Public Education," PA Schools Work, accessed Nov 11, 2025, paschoolswork.org/pennsylvania-drops-to-45th-in-the-nation-in-state-funding-for-public-education.

55 **In 2014, low-income:** "Complaint Summary," Fund Our Schools PA, accessed November 11, 2025, elc-pa.org/wp-content/uploads/2014/11/PAFundingSuit_Executive_Summary.pdf.

56 **"This is an earthquake":** Maddie Hanna, Kristen A. Graham, and Gillian McGoldrick, "Landmark Pa. School Funding Case Decided: The State's System is Unconstitutional," *The Philadelphia Inquirer*, February 7, 2023, inquirer.com/news/school-funding-lawsuit-pennsylvania-result-20230207.html.

56 **A 2022 index by the Century Foundation:** Dale Mezzacappa, "Philadelphia Area Schools Among the Most Segregated in the Country," Chalkbeat Philadelphia, May 23, 2022, philadelphia.chalkbeat.org/2022/5/23/23137855/philadelphia-area-schools-among-most-segregated-country.

56 **In 2025, spending per weighted student:** "School Funding Data," PA Schools Work website, accessed August 14, 2025, paschoolswork.org/school-district-data.

The Suburban Strategy

100 **"Ours is a community":** Neil A. Sheehan, "Wallingford-Swarthmore Appeals for Calm in Wake of Racist Incidents," *Delco Daily Times*, January 3, 2019, delcotimes.com/2019/01/03/wallingford-swarthmore-appeals-for-calm-in-wake-of-racist-incidents.

Home Going

109 **"Within one generation, a people":** James N. Gregory, "The Second Great Migration: An Historical Overview," in *African American Urban History: The Dynamics of Race, Class and Gender since World War II.*, ed. Joe W. Trotter Jr. and Kenneth L. Kusmer (University of Chicago Press, 2009).

109 **At the end of World War II:** Kelly Simpson, "The Great Migration: Creating a New Black Identity in Los Angeles," PBS SoCal, February 15, 2012, kcet.org/history-society/the-great-migration-creating-a-new-black-identity-in-los-angeles.

115 **"I come here this evening":** Robert F. Kennedy, "Day of Affirmation" Address, University of Cape Town, Cape Town, South Africa, June 6, 1966, John F. Kennedy Presidential Library and Museum website, accessed August 10, 2025, jfklibrary.org/learn/about-jfk/the-kennedy-family/robert-f-kennedy/robert-f-kennedy-speeches/day-of-affirmation-address-university-of-capetown-capetown-south-africa-june-6-1966.

122 **Culver City was founded:** "Tourists and newcomers are specially invited. This is your opportunity to see Culver City at our expense—the Culver City that you've heard about. See this model little white city, scarcely a year and a half old. Learn the interesting history of

this growth—a growth that has been the talk of Southern California." Advertisements column 1, *Los Angeles Herald*, Volume XLI, Number 113, March 12, 1915, cdnc.ucr.edu/?a=d&d=LAH19150312.2.179.1.

134 **You will notice most:** Monica Davalos and Sara Kimberlin, "Who Is Experiencing Homelessness in California?," California Budget and Policy Center, March 2023, calbudgetcenter.org/resources/who-is-experiencing-homelessness-in-california.

Freedom, Pt. 2

172 **"Many of us have been":** "A call to action!" Accountability at VONA, accessed September 16, 2025, via Internet Archive Wayback Machine, web.archive.org/web/20210227045920/https://accountabilityatvona.com.

173 **"As the night progressed":** Marianella Belliard, "Junot Díaz's Mask: This Is How He Lost It (OPINION)," Latino Rebels, May 10, 2018, latinorebels.com/2018/05/10/junotdiazsmask.

173 **"Each night together":** Shreerekha, "In the Wake of His Damage," *The Rumpus*, May 12, 2018, therumpus.net/2018/05/12/in-the-wake-of-his-damage.

173 **"And maybe he did":** Alisa Valdes, "I Tried to Warn You About Junot Díaz," Tremenda Manguita & Other Magnetisms: Verbal Periphrastics from the Discursive Depths of Writer/Producer Alisa Valdes, May 4, 2018, accessed via Internet Archive Wayback Machine, web.archive.org/web/20180526134136/https://oshuncreative.wordpress.com/2018/05/04/i-tried-to-warn-you-about-junot-diaz.

A People Without a Nation

195 **"Blacks must sit as one":** Steve Biko, "Black Consciousness and the Quest for True Humanity," in *I Write What I Like*: *Selected Writings*, ed. Aelred Stubbs C.R. (University of Chicago Press, 2024), Kindle.

196 **"The Blacks of the Americas":** Orlando Patterson, "Toward a Future That Has No Past—Reflections on the Fate of Blacks in the Americas," *The Public Interest* 27 (Spring 1972): 60–61.

197 **"The slave ship is":** Saidiya Hartman, "The Belly of the World: A Note on Black Women's Labors," *Souls* 18, no. 1 (2016): 166.

197 **"This boat is a womb":** Édouard Glissant, "The Open Boat," in *Poetics of Relation*, trans. Betsy Wing (University of Michigan Press, 1997), 5–6.

198 **"In many ways":** Saidiya V. Hartman and Frank B. Wilderson III, "The Position of the Unthought," interview by Frank B. Wilderson III, *Qui Parle* 13, no. 2 (Spring/Summer 2003): 185.

199 **"Why is anti-Black violence":** Frank B. Wilderson III, *Afropessimism* (Liveright, 2020), 17.

199 **In 2020, *The New York Times*:** kihana miraya ross, "Call It What It Is: Anti-Blackness," *The New York Times*, Opinion, June 4, 2020.

199 **And even *Forbes* ran:** Janice Gassam Asare, PhD, "Recognizing and Dismantling Your Anti-Blackness," *Forbes*, June 1, 2020, forbes.com/sites/janicegassam/2020/06/01/recognizing-and-dismantling-your-anti-blackness.

200 **"Like the related terms 'affect'":** Jesse McCarthy, "On Afropessimism," *Los Angeles Review of Books*, July 20, 2020, lareviewofbooks.org/article/on-afropessimism.

201 **In the early 1940s:** Douglas Field, "James Baldwin's Life on the Left: A Portrait of the Artist as a Young New York Intellectual," *ELH - English Literary History* 78, no. 4 (Winter 2011): 849.

202 **His 1947 review:** Field, "James Baldwin's Life on the Left," 850.

202 ***The New Leader* and *Partisan Review*:** Field, "James Baldwin's Life on the Left," 855.

203 **in *Partisan Review* and finally in *Perspectives USA*:** Field, "James Baldwin's Life on the Left," 857.

203 **The film garnered:** Troy Patterson, "A New Adaptation of 'Native Son' Reaches the Limits of What the Text Has to Offer," *The New Yorker*, April 5, 2019, newyorker.com/culture/on-television/a-new-adaptation-of-native-son-reaches-the-limits-of-what-the-text-has-to-offer.

203 **"Now that I've read":** Imani Perry, "The Bleak Prescience of Richard Wright," *The Atlantic*, June 2021, theatlantic.com/magazine/archive/2021/06/richard-wright-man-who-lived-underground/618705.

204 **"The Bigger Thomases were":** Richard Wright, "How 'Bigger' Was Born," in *Native Son* (Harper Perennial Modern Classics, 1998), 437.

205 **"From far away Nazi Germany":** Wright, "How 'Bigger' Was Born," 446.

207 **Robinson devotes an entire chapter:** Cedric J. Robinson, *Black Marxism: The Making of the Black Radical Tradition* (University of North Carolina Press, 1983), 5.

207 **"He was never merely":** Robinson, *Black Marxism*, 290.

208 **"But getting rid of social death":** Frank B. Wilderson III, "The Year Afropessimism Hit the Streets?: A Conversation at the Edge of the World," interview by Aaron Robertson, *Lit Hub*, August 27, 2020, lithub.com/the-year-afropessimism-hit-the-streets-a-conversation-at-the-edge-of-the-world.

210 **The study, confidently touted:** Sean McElwee and Jason McDaniel, "Economic Anxiety Didn't Make People Vote Trump, Racism Did," *The Nation*, May 8, 2017, thenation.com/article/archive/economic-anxiety-didnt-make-people-vote-trump-racism-did.

211 **The study does not account:** Pew Research Center, "For Most Trump Voters, 'Very Warm' Feelings for Him Endured," August 2018, 16, pewresearch.org/politics/wp-content/uploads/sites/4/2018/08/8-9-2018-Validated-voters-release-with-10-2-19-and-10-17-18-corrections.pdf.

212 **for a literature of engagement:** Richard Wright, "Blueprint for Negro Writing (1937)," in *Within the Circle: An Anthology of African American Literary Criticism from the Harlem Renaissance to the Present*, ed. Angelyn Mitchell (Duke University Press, 1994), 106.

213 **"White" is not a fixed:** James Baldwin, "On Being White . . . and Other Lies," in *James Baldwin: The Cross of Redemption*, ed. Randall Kenan (Pantheon Books, 2010).

214 **"Democrats have no unsullied history":** Toni Morrison, "Racism and Fascism," in *The Source of Self-Regard* (Alfred A. Knopf, 2019), 15.

Coda

219 ***Just because we don't*:** "Full interview: Witnesses Respond to Stabbing in Davis," video, 3:40, in Daniel Macht, "Woman in Critical Condition After 3rd Davis Stabbing in 5 Days; Search for Suspect," KCRA, May 2, 2023, kcra.com/article/shelter-in-place-ordered-in-downtown-davis-after-reports-of-3rd-stabbing/43766172.

219 ***We moved from Lebanon*:** Brittany Hope, "Father of Slain UC Davis Student Honors Son: 'Full of Ambition, Proud of his Roots,'"

KCRA, May 2, 2023, kcra.com/article/uc-davis-student-fatally-stabbed-father-speaks/43759842.

220 ***We started sleeping in groups*:** "Full Interview," at 0:51, in Macht, "Woman in Critical Condition."

220 **We learn that the killer:** Matthew Miranda and Steven Hobbs, "Who Is Carlos Dominguez? Suspected Davis Killer Grew Up in Oakland, Football Team Captain," *Sacramento Bee*, May 10, 2023.

220 ***He had said that*:** Brittney Mejia, "Athlete, Honor Student, Murderer? How Did a UC Davis Student Spiral into an Accused Killer?," *Los Angeles Times*, August 10, 2023.

220 ***We need to be protected*:** "Full Interview," at 3:38, in Macht, "Woman in Critical Condition."